Teacher's

General Certificate English

New Edition

ALAN ETHERTON

Nelson

Thomas Nelson & Sons Ltd
Nelson House Mayfield Road
Walton-on-Thames Surrey
KT12 5PL   UK

Thomas Nelson Australia
102 Dodds Street
South Melbourne
Victoria 3205 Australia

Nelson Canada
1120 Birchmount Road
Scarborough Ontario
MIK 5G4 Canada

© Alan Etherton 1994

First edition published by Thomas Nelson & Sons Ltd 1983
Second edition published by Thomas Nelson & Sons Ltd 1987

I(T)P Thomas Nelson is an International Thomson Publishing Company

I(T)P is used under licence

ISBN 0-17-433327-7
NPN 9 8 7 6 5 4 3

All rights reserved. No paragraph of this publication may be reproduced, copied or transmitted save with written permission or in accordance with the provisions of the Copyright, Design and Patents Act 1988, or under the terms of any licence permitting limited copying issued by the Copyright Licensing Agency, 90 Tottenham Court Road, London W1P 9HE.

Any person who does any unauthorised act in relation to this publication may be liable to criminal prosecution and civil claims for damages.

Printed in Croatia.

Contents

Part 1: Summary
2	What the examiners say	1
3	Summary: practice passage 1	1
4	Making notes: practice passage 2	2
5	Extracting information, passage 3	2
6	Practice passage 4	3
7	Practice passage 5	3
9	Making a summary of Letters 2	4
10	Practice passage 6	4
11	Practice passage 7	5
12	Practice passage 8	5

Part 2: Comprehension, Summary & Directed Writing
13	Figurative language	7
14	Answering vocabulary questions	7
15	Obstacles to understanding	8
16	Practice passage 1	9
17	Practice passage 2A	10
18	Practice passages 2B and 2C	10
19	Practice passage 3	11
20	Types of comprehension questions	12
21	Practice passage 4	12
23	Practice passage 5	14
24	Practice passage 6	15
25	Practice passage 7	15
26	Practice passage 8	16
27	Practice passages 9 and 10	17
28	Practice passage 11	18
29	Practice passage 12	19
30	Practice passage 13	20
31	Practice passage 14	21
32	Practice passage 15	25
33	Practice passage 16	25
34	Practice passage 17	26
35	Understanding situations	27

Part 3: Communication in writing: Composition
36	Communication in writing	29
37	Composition – basic points	30
41	Finishing a composition	30
42	What kind of English shall I use?	31
43	Further practice with basic skills	31

Part 4: Vocabulary
54	Words in context	33
55	Antonyms, synonyms & homonyms	34
56	Pairs of words	35
57	Phrasal verbs	36
58	Prefixes and meaning	38
59	Problem words & correct usage 1	39
60	Problem Words & correct usage 2	39
61	Idioms and common expressions	40
62	Common errors	43

Part 5: Language Practice
63	Word formation & parts of speech	44
64	Adjectives	45
65	Agreement	46
66	Articles	46
67	Cloze passages	47
68	Comparison	48
69	Conditionals and 'If'	48
70	Connectives	49
71	Future action	50
72	Gerunds	50
73	Indirect (reported) speech	51
74	Indirect (reported) questions	52
75	Infinitives	53
76	Participles	54
77	Prepositions	55
78	Pronouns	56
79	Punctuation	57
80	Spelling	58
81	Verbs: present tenses	59
82	Verbs: past actions	59

Preface

This key has been written for use with the new edition of General Certificate English by Dr Alan Etherton. The original book was revised in 1994 to take into account (a) changes made in the GCE syllabuses and (b) current examination papers. The Key includes answers to most exercises (including summary questions) but does not include specimen compositions because these are not permitted by examining authorities who have given permission for past questions to be included in the student's textbook. The answers to all past examination questions are the author's own assessment of what is required and are not answers supplied by the examining authorities.

The author will be happy to answer any queries or to hear of any way of improving this book (in future editions) if teachers would like to write to him c/o Thomas Nelson & Sons Ltd., Nelson House, Mayfield Road, Walton-on-Thames, Surrey KT12 5PL, England.

Part 1: Summary

2 What the examiners say

Copies of past papers and examiners' reports can be obtained from:
(University of London)
ULEAC Publications, Unit 3, River Park Industrial Estate, Billet Lane, Berkhamsted, Hertfordshire, HP4 1EL, U.K.
(University of Cambridge)
Local Examinations Syndicate, 1 Hills Road, Cambridge CB1 2EU, U.K.

Exercise 1, page 4
1 c   2 d   3 a

Exercise 2, page 6
1   Many vehicles use King's Road daily.
2   Most traffic accidents are probably caused by inexcusable carelessness.
3   Girls now have a good chance of success in various careers.
4   Nature has given each creature a means of defence.

Exercise 3, page 7
1 b   2 c   3 a   4 b   5 b

Exercise 4, page 8
1   Carelessness causes accidents.
2   Many careers are open to girls.
3   Many vehicles use King's Road.
4   A recession affects all countries.
5   The price of petrol has risen in recent years.
6   Despite research into AIDS, no cure has yet been found for it.
7   The airport is so crowded with tourists that a new one is needed.
8   Sometimes workers are afraid of losing their jobs because of mechanization.
9   A man found some abandoned cubs in the forest, so he took them to his camp.

3 Summary – practice passage 1

Questions, page 11
1 b   2 a   3 b   4 d   5 c

Questions, page 13
1   It is information not given in a passage but brought in from outside.
2   No.
3   These were unnecessary details.
4   They got this material from the passage. They were wrong to include these items

but they probably did so because they could not understand what the whole passage was about.
5 Yes.

4 Making notes – practice passage 2

If we rely solely on the notes, we have this summary:
   Men help to cause deserts in various ways. Primitive methods of farming take the goodness out of the soil. Grazing and goats cause further deterioration and no plants are left. When timber is cut on the hills, erosion and flooding follow. Lack of irrigation increases salinity in the soil and reduces crops. Dams deprive the land of silt and do not remove salt deposits (which harm the soil). In addition, the increasing population has led to over-intensive cultivation, which has caused further erosion on hills.
   Nature can also help to create deserts. Rain leads to erosion and floods. Droughts and strong winds can remove topsoil …
(At this point, I must pause to count up the words. I want to see whether I must stop quickly or add more words to reach an acceptable length. I find that the total is 105. I cannot conveniently add another 40 words, so I must re-write the summary, padding it out as I go.)

   Both men and nature have acted to turn good land into desert. Various factors have been involved. Primitive methods of farming have taken the goodness out of the soil. Grazing and the keeping of goats have caused further deterioration to the point at which no plants are left. When timber is cut on the hills, erosion and flooding are likely to follow. Lack of irrigation can increase salinity in the soil, thereby reducing the amount of food obtained from crops. Dams deprive the land of fertile silt and do not remove the salt deposits which harm the soil. In addition, the steady increase in the population has led to over-intensive cultivation, and this has caused further erosion on hills.
(It is time to count again. This time I have used 119 words. I must expand the 19 words in the second paragraph of the first draft. I need to use another 30 words or so.)

Nature can also help to create deserts in various ways. Heavy rain can lead to serious erosion and damaging floods. Droughts and strong winds can strip away the topsoil.
(Total: 148 words)

5 Extracting information – practice passage 3

Questions, page 19

1) I would omit *postage stamp, adhesive stamp, varieties* and *classics*. Yes, it is necessary to number the kinds of stamps. This is required in the instructions.
2) We have to use not more than 80 words and give reasons for issuing and collecting. My draft summary (based on the notes) is:

Originally, stamps were issued as a receipt for the handling and delivery of mail. Later on, they were used to show life in a country and to commemorate important or international events. In due course, special stamps were used for airmail postage. In more recent times, stamps have been issued primarily to obtain money from stamp-collectors. *(It is time to count words. I have used 56 words so far, so I can use only 24 more words in the last paragraph. The notes consist of about 15 words, so I cannot add very much.)*

2

People collect stamps mainly for pleasure and interest. They learn about the world and are interested in varieties, thematics, sheets and first-day covers. However, stamp-collecting can also be an investment.

(The total length is now 86 words, which is too long. To keep within the limit of 80 words, I will omit 'In due course' and change 'In more recent times' to 'Recently'. Then I have my final summary.)

6 Practice passage 4

This is a good question because it will be easy for students who have learnt how to make a summary but very difficult for those who rely on copying from a passage. An examiner will use a check-list similar to this one:

A female (*Anopheles*) mosquito can carry a malaria parasite and transmit the disease when it bites a mammal and sucks blood from it.

The mosquito then lays its eggs in standing water. The eggs soon hatch and eventually become mosquitoes.

Malaria is a dangerous disease but it is not caught in Britain.

Travellers to tropical countries in Africa and Asia may be at risk, especially at dawn and dusk, when mosquitoes are most active.

The risk is reduced if you cover as much skin as possible and take the recommended anti-malaria tablets.

If you do catch malaria, get medical treatment immediately.

Malaria can cause an abortion, so pregnant women should be very careful.

Normally the marking scheme used by assistant examiners will include a check-list so that examiners can award a mark for each of the listed points.

In this particular question, candidates have to remember that their leaflet will be read by overseas travellers from Britain.

7 Practice passage 5

Questions, page 23

a) We are told in the instructions that 'most of these points can be expressed in a single word', so it might be wise to shorten the items given on page 23, when this is possible. We can combine some points and have this list:

   1 choice of topic   6 coherence
   2 arrangement of ideas   7 freedom from errors
   3 planning and unity   8 punctuation
   4 courtesy, good handwriting 9 idioms
   5 correct language   10 checking

b) The summary should contain these points. They are given here as a list for convenience in checking students' summaries. (Put the task and length at the top of the notes so that we know what we are looking for and how long the notes should be.)

Information about reader. (100 words – notes 40–60)
probably different age and background from writer

3

becomes learner when marking essays
may be from different country and anxious to learn
expects well-planned presentation of ideas
entitled to courtesy in writing and to correct language
accepts lower standard than own but expects clear meaning

9 Making a summary of letters 2

An outline of the summary will be:

Mary Downton wrote to a newspaper to urge that the Form 5 examination should be abolished. Writing as a mother, she said ...
 too much pressure in Forms 3–5
 students spend more time on sports, TV
 results not reliable
 some subjects not useful
 need more relevant material
 revise syllabuses

A teenager, John Stocker, replied to Mrs Downton's letter and said ... disagreed
 agreed – revise syllabuses, include current topics
 exams vital as stimulus – make students work hard
 exams needed for public recognition of achievements
 improve but don't destroy exams

10 Practice passage 6

Questions, pages 31–32

1 In addition to climbing problems (which were overcome by using skill and cooperation), the climbers had to use oxygen to make breathing possible. Since their supply of oxygen was limited, they had to maintain reasonable progress so that they did not run out of oxygen. In addition, the climb proved to be a mental strain but they met this with resolve and determination.

2 (Does 'equipment' include flags and food?) Perhaps we should mention these in case they are on the examiner's list of items.)

In addition to flags and food, the climbers took masks and oxygen bottles to enable them to breathe. They had axes or other cutting equipment, as well as rope and a camera. Presumably, they also had warm clothing.

3 We know that the author's reactions were numbed because he tells us that his mind seemed almost to have ceased to function. He climbed automatically and did not realise that he was on Everest and without oxygen. He felt insensible to the exertion of climbing and at one time could not talk or think.

4 At first the author was disoriented (because of the effort and lack of oxygen). After he reached the top, his spirit seemed at first to become detached from his body. When he recovered control of his senses and body, he became extremely emotional – both outwardly and inwardly. Then he experienced a powerful feeling of what he calls 'completeness', which was certainly the result of a supreme achievement.

5   (Both Passages)
(Does 'in the final stage of the climb' refer to the climb to the peak or the descent? Since Passage 2 says nothing about the descent, we must assume it refers to the climb towards the top.)

In Passage 1, Hillary is calm, controlled and confident of success. He shows no signs of strain or great stress and is able to climb upwards methodically. The writer of the second passage shows quite different behaviour. He is very weak physically, collapsing every few steps. He is no longer in full control of his mind or body, and climbs automatically.

11 Practice passage 7

1   a) (At first sight, it is not clear whether the 'results' include some of the information under 'The findings'. However, it is clear from 1(b) that we are not meant to be dealing with 'the findings' in 1(a). This shows the need for students to read all the summary/directed writing questions which refer to a particular passage, so that they can quickly see to which section(s) of the passage each question refers.)

The surveys revealed that most fatal accidents involving cyclists were the result of a collision with a vehicle or train. Many cyclists showed poor riding skills or were unable to control a bicycle well. Younger children were particularly vulnerable. The accidents led to fatal head injuries and other injuries.

b) Bicycle accidents can be reduced if parents ensure that children are taught to ride well and that they wear safety helmets. Children below the age of twelve should not be allowed on busy roads. Schools can help by requiring pupils to pass a proficiency test before riding to school. Manufacturers should increase the safety of bicycles, especially by providing a carrier for school bags. Highway authorities can help by providing separate cycle paths to keep cyclists away from vehicles.

2   (Many answers are possible, since the speech merely uses the article as a starting point and is not restricted to the facts in the article.)

12 Practice passage 8

1   (a) (You may like to discuss this question with your students. From time to time, examiners set questions which are either ambiguous or are unclear. This is one of those occasions!)

Are students meant to describe only the volcano or what they might have seen of human activity while watching the volcano? If the examiners expect only an account of the volcano, why does the question refer to lines 1–18 and 32–44, although much of the material in these two sections is **not** concerned with the volcano directly? If the examiners wanted only an account of volcanic activity, the relevant lines are, 1–6, 12, (possibly) and 38–44 . My own reaction was to look again at 1(b) and q.2 to see if there was a separate question about the people and their boats. Since there isn't, I am forced to play safe and include something about them in my answer. My answer might then be along these lines:

At first I saw smoke pouring from the volcano and red-hot cinders shooting into the sky with a low roar. Later on, the smoke had become black, the air was full of flying ash, and the volcano was making much more noise as rocks and fiery flames shot out.

Two broad streams of burning lava poured down towards the sea. (60 words)

*I also saw people getting things from their homes, and men launching four boats. (14 words)

*I have added this sentence because I happened to notice them while I was watching the volcano. (The question does not indicate whether we should include or omit this information.)

What the examiners said

In their report on this examination, the examiners said:

"Q.1(a) is a summary, in this case, of approximately 100 words. It was not a story, but invited an account of the eruption before its full activity and at its worst. Too many candidates misread the question and told a large part of the story or copied out a mixture of relevance and irrelevance. Too few heard little of the volcano but just the shrieking of people and they misread the quieter low roar of the beginning compared with the later explosions. It would be wise to train candidates to read carefully, and to work out exactly what to do."

1 b) Any four of these feelings (written as complete sentences):
awe – smoke and red-hot cinders from volcano
sense of urgency – homes and lives threatened
stunned (moved like automatons) – unexpected and nowhere to flee
desperate – trying to escape by boat
sad – loss of animals = worldly wealth
weary – walk up to the top of the cliff
astonished – power of the volcano

What the examiners said

'Candidates were asked for four feelings and evidence for each answer. Often the feelings were not clearly identified and the evidence was offered amongst narrative. Again this was a summary-type which was sometimes misunderstood as an opportunity to write a story.'

Moral: Students should be rehearsed in the types of questions they are likely to meet and how to tackle them.

    c) The examiners said: 'This was an extension of the story that needed some good description of the volcano seen from the sea and of what the villagers felt about escaping from their island for good. 'Next' was not always understood, so that there was more re-telling and frequently copying out of the story. Those who continued it wrote in a reasonably descriptive style and used the ideas in the text moderately well.'

But notice that to be able to write about an escape from the island, students would need to take into account the introduction before line 1. Without this, they would not know that the islanders had escaped.

Part 2: Comprehension, Summary and Directed Writing

13 Figurative language

Exercise 1, page 38
1. (a) figuratively – beat him easily (b) literally
2. (a) literally (b) figuratively – revise or review
3. (a) figuratively – conceited (b) literally
4. (a) figuratively – searched thoroughly (b) literally
5. (a) figuratively – obstacle (b) literally
6. (a) literally (b) figuratively – boyfriend; person available
7. (a) figuratively – person of hidden quality. A rough diamond is somebody whose manners or appearance may seem rough but who means well and has good qualities. (b) literally
8. (a) literally (b) figuratively. We say that a person's heart sinks when he or she is affected by feelings of despair, gloom or even fear.
9. (a) figuratively – suddenly (became angry) (b) literally
10. (a) figuratively – a person who will drive a hard bargain and possible cheat you (b) literally

Exercise 2, page 40
In this and many other exercises in the book, there are many alternatives.

1. a crab with rheumatism
2. a snail with a headache
3. a frightened rabbit
4. a starving dog
5. a cucumber
6. a baby
7. a fox
8. two spoilt children

14 Answering vocabulary questions

Exercise 1, page 42
1. recently
2. scarcely, only just
3. scarcely, only with difficulty
4. impressed
5. cold, intimidating, hostile
6. lenient; a strong means of enforcement
7. something intended to conceal his real feelings; capable of working out what is in his best interests
8. enthusiastic and active; wishing to preserve things
9. unlawful, illegal
10. except, other than
11. always. The word is often used to mean 'nearly always'.
12. not good because of lack of use

Exercise 2, page 42

1. figuratively
2. figuratively
3. literally
4. figuratively
5. literally
6. figuratively
7. figuratively
8. literally
9. literally
10. figuratively

Exercise 3, page 43

1. This word means that Mary said the accident was John's fault. 'Blamed' means 'said it was his own fault'.
2. The expression means 'process by process'. This expression tells us that the manager explained successive stages in the production process.
3. This means 'make him conscious again'.
4. The expression means 'became conscious again'.
5. This expression means 'nobody was watching, so they could proceed safely'.
6. 'Nevertheless' means 'in spite of this fact'.
   'For the time being' means 'at the present moment'.
7. This expression means 'alternatively'.
8. Here 'boosting' means 'improving and giving a stimulus to'. 'Creating' means 'making'.
9. A common illness is one which is widespread or occurs frequently.
10. Here, 'tempted' means 'nearly persuaded'.

Exercise 4, page 44

1. blamed
2. neat
3. unconscious
4. We
5. by means of a path through the mountains
6. for the time being
7. may
8. one way
9. tempted
10. another (or 'employer')

Exercise 5, page 45

1. unanticipated
2. experienced
3. against
4. down payment
5. vital
6. bad
7. sufficient
8. lack of respect for
9. influence
10. grateful

Exercise 6, page 46

1. investigate
2. increased
3. past
4. completely broken
5. has
6. gone
7. As a result
8. temporarily

15 Obstacles to understanding

I Passive and active verbs

Test

1. A player.
2. A player
3. A spectator.
4. A spectator.

16 Practice passage 1

1(a) (i) They had to wait until Lord John called them up. In addition, they were delayed by one of the professors who stopped to admire a flower or insect.
 (ii) There were four people on the expedition.
 (iii) It tells us that the area of brushwood was long and thin in shape.
 (b) (i) strewn with boulders (? tangle of rocks)
 "Strewn with boulders" is better because of the word 'large' in the question.
 (ii) He moved in a 'stooping and running' way so that he would not be seen and would get to the place as quickly as possible.
 (iii) At first, he was too astonished at what he had seen to think about waving to the others to advance.
 (c) (i) The pit may have been a volcanic blow-hole, i.e. a hole through which gases or other substances had escaped under pressure.
 (ii) We are told that the pit was hundreds of metres deep. Since it was bowl-shaped, it was probably hundreds of metres in diameter too.

2(a) (i) Two of the following:
  1 The creatures laid eggs and the females hatched them.
  2 They looked like birds.
  3 They had wings.
  4 They guarded and defended their nests and young.
 (ii) They used their eyes to watch for intruders. Since the creatures could make babbling and whistling noises, they could presumably hear an intruder approaching.
 (b) The men inferred from the remains of fish that the creatures were likely to live near the sea. This explained why fossils of them had been found in coastal areas.
 (c) The pterodactyls had risen higher and higher, so they appeared smaller.
 (d) Any five of:
  1 non-stop
  2 motionless
  3 having round its edges
  4 horrible to look at
  5 except for
  6 fascinated
  7 withdraw
  8 enthusiasm

3 (This is a very strange question since a pterodactyl could probably not reason as a human being can, and certainly could not speak or write. Adventurous students might enjoy themselves writing this account!)

A possible answer would probably contain the following points (but arranged in continuous prose):

Something moved at the edge of the pit, and I …
saw a weird monkey-like creature watching us.
I whistled to warn my colleagues.
We flew over and around the four intruders,
and gradually drew nearer to them.
They retreated to the forest but we
dived and attacked them.
We hit three of them and knocked two of them down.
One of the enemy wounded my second cousin and broke one of his wings.

We attacked again and knocked one monster down but
they escaped into the trees.
We flew round for some time
to make sure that they did not return.

17 Practice passage 2A

(a) Mr Brimlow – Luther's father
Mrs Brimlow – Luther's mother
Mr Armroyd – Luther's employer
Mr Pentecost – one of Luther's neighbours (with a complaint about Luther)
Mrs Pentecost – another of Luther's neighbours
the writer – a son or daughter of the Pentecosts and a neighbour of Luther's
(b) (i) only just
    (ii) scarcely (to a very limited extent)
(c) When a person borrows something, he intends to return it, but in the case of theft he intends to deprive the owner of it.
(d) her narrow cunning face
sniffing danger like a vixen
(e) The Pentecosts had called at the Brimlows' house to complain of something which Luther had done. If Mr Armroyd heard about this, he might change his mind and go to the police.
(f) theft
(g) pale and trembling
licked his lips
began to babble
(h) Instead of complaining to the police, he had taken Luther home to explain to his parents what he had done wrong.

18 Practice passages 2B and 2C

Passage 2B, page 58

(i) (i) astonishment (surprise)
    (ii) He was astonished when Mrs Brimlow said that he had written letters praising Luther, when in fact he had not written any letters. He was very surprised because Mrs Brimlow was referring to letters which he had not written.
(j) They had been forged by Luther.
(k) In lines 40–41, it is suggested that he had been stealing money from the petty cash account in Mr Armroyd's office.
(l) (i) be successful (make a name for himself)
    (ii) try to make yourself appear more successful
(m) Instead of becoming angry, he somewhat admired the forgery and kept control of himself.

Passage 2C, page 59

(n) (i) occurred to
    (ii) living at too high a standard or being too ambitious
    (iii) honesty
(o) (i) sums

10

        (ii) considerable (for a long time)
        (iii) travels first class
        (iv) stop your tongue clacking
        (v) a prodigy
    (p) He had paid him more money than his position merited.

Vocabulary, page 60

1 B, D
2 A (B does not explain 'thoroughly'.)
3 C, D
4 B
5 D
6 C, D
7 B
8 C, D
9 C
10 A
11 B
12 C
13 B
14 – (mean)
15 B
16 A, perhaps B
17 A
18 C

19 Practice passage 3

Questions, pages 63–65

(a) The ship was killing many whales, the whales were too small, and the ship was operating in a part of the sea where it was not supposed to be.
(b) (i) trying to conceal its activities
    (ii) protection of living things
(c) He wanted to obtain information about ships which might be illegally killing whales, and by subscribing to Lloyd's he could get this information.
(d) A conservation group, 'Greenpeace', had earlier alleged that the *Sierra* was involved in illegal whale-catching, and records of the ship were held by the computer.
(e) (i) In the first question, he wanted to find out whether a freighter was accompanying the *Sierra*. When this failed, he asked whether a freighter ever met the *Sierra*. When this failed, he asked whether a freighter ever met the *Sierra* in a port.
    (ii) He knew that the *Sierra* would transfer its catch to a refrigerated ship, so he wanted to find out when the two ships met.
    (iii) He wanted to know where he might be able to catch the *Sierra* transferring its catch and thus have clear evidence of illegal activities.
(f) The whale meat would go bad unless it could be put in refrigerated holds, and this would also enable the *Sierra* to continue with its task of killing whales.
(g) He wanted to find out if a ship was waiting for the *Sierra* and where it was waiting.
(h) (i) He still wanted to get more specific information.
    (ii) This produced some very useful information for Brown.
(i) He wanted to be able to get into the guarded docks easily, and his disguise made the guards think that he was a harmless fisherman.
(j) They proved that the ship had caught and killed whales and was transferring the meat to a Japanese ship.
(k) unwelcome people
(l) They enabled him to get near enough to take significant photographs, one of which showed the nature of the goods being transferred. They also got him a copy of the ship's manifest, proving that it was carrying whale meat.
(m) This is not clear from the passage because the 'loading' (in line 62) appears to refer to the *Yamato Reefer* rather than to the *Sierra*, which was unloading. However, if the reference is to the *Sierra*, we can say that the crew notified the

harbour police, stopped loading and moved the ship to a more remote and inaccessible part of the harbour.

Multiple-choice questions, page 66

(i) (4) is wrong because it is not a sentence.
    (1) does not clearly explain why he pretended to be a fisherman.
    (3) is shorter than (2). Both are correct but (3) is perhaps better because it is easier to write.
(j) (1) is factually wrong and inadequate.
    (2) is inadequate.
    (3) is wrong because there is no proof that the *Sierra* was Japanese.
    (4) is correct.
(k) (1) This is factually and grammatically wrong.
    (2) Untrue.
    (3) Correct.
    (4) Untrue.

20 Types of comprehension questions

1. Luther had been travelling first class, he had worn expensive clothes and he had eaten at expensive restaurants.
He did not know where to find the *Sierra* at first. It was difficult for him to get into the docks, and the ship moved before he could finish taking his first lot of photographs.
2. They showed indifference or even hostility towards each other. He uses 'even' to emphasise the fact that the ship's name was known.
3. (i) ashamed (ii) conciliatory persistence
4. He probably realised that Luther was more skilful and unscrupulous than he had suspected, and this made him even more determined to make Luther leave the city. He probably became more excited and pleased when he managed to trace the ship and get definite evidence. He probably became increasingly angry with the owners of the ship, too.
5. (i) Yes (ii) Yes (iii) No (iv) No
6. 'That man may be working for the Press. Make sure he doesn't find out what we're doing.'
'I went to the home of one of our junior clerks to warn his parents that he had been stealing money from our petty cash. I discovered that the boy have been forging letters, and I think his parents now know what they boy is really like, so the visit wasn't a complete waste of time.'
7–10 These are merely specimen questions and do not refer to a particular passage.
11. information (It refers to information from Lloyd's.)
12. (3), 1. He sympathises with the peasants.
    2. He implies that action ought to have been taken to prevent the situation.

21 Practice passage 4

Questions, page 71

(a) (i) year after year without any change
    (ii) most important of all the factors

(iii) except
(iv) provided with food by
(b) It refers to growing food.
(c) He could cause the river to flood and cover the crops.
(d) accurate
(e) (i) and (ii) are related, so it is better to prepare the rough answers for both sections together. They can then be separated to provide the two answers.
    (i) Any ten of the following:

1	fertile land	9	a blacksmith
2	reasonable temperature	10	granaries or barns
3	not exposed to the wind	11	guards or a defence
4	not in the shadow of trees	12	planning for growing
5	not too swampy	13	people who know weather and calendar
6	water		
7	tools	14	roads or tracks
8	oxen or horses	15	market supervision

Note: The question asks about things which are necessary, so I would omit items such as (9) and (15) which are not mentioned as being essential.

    (ii) Any ten of the following:

1	grow crops	8	pull a plough
2	good growing conditions	9	make and repair tools
3	crops not damaged by the wind	10	store the crops
		11	protect the settlement
4	crops can grow well	12	work in the right seasons
5	soil not waterlogged	13	do things at the right time
6	crops can grow	14	communications for market
7	cultivate the soil	15	check market facilities

Note: If I had time in an examination, I would rewrite some of the points in (i) and (ii) to use the full six words allowed and make the points clearer to the reader.

(f) practice (line 29)
(g) (i) He uses 'even' to show that schools are not needed. The use of 'even' stresses his surprise.
    (ii) He uses 'even' to do this.

Note: I fell into a simple trap in answering these questions. I read (i) without reading (ii) and thus gave the answer to both (i) and (ii) in my answer to (i). This demonstrates the need for students to read all parts of this type of question before answering the first part. A similar situation arose in (e).

(h) 1   The same kinds of crops are grown
    2   To obtain crops, a similar routine is followed each year.
    3   The sequence of events is identical each year.
    4   People do the same work each year.

Note: I did not notice that we must use six words only, so I must change these answers to shorter ones:

    The same crops are grown.
    2   A similar growing routine is followed.
    3   The annual sequence does not change.
    4   People do the same work annually.

If time permits, students need practice in reducing 8–12 words to a smaller number of words, as shown above.

(i) (The answer may be in lines 38–39 but it is wise to include all available evidence from the passage if this can be done.)

We are told that this might be done by wild animals, floods or attacks by neighbouring or other people.

(j) (This type of question is known as 'Directed Writing'. It arises from something in the passage but is *not* necessarily a summary or paraphrase. We can use some points from the answer to (e). The *key word* in this question is *differs*, so it would be wrong merely to describe life in any town.)

Town life is not as conservative as that of an agricultural community. People in towns do not have to depend on the soil, the availability of water in the immediate vicinity, a favourable climate, the use of animals or experts familiar with the agricultural calendar. They probably need greater division of labour and better roads. They also need reservoirs and an excellent defence system. The people need manufacturing and service industries to provide employment and they are much more accustomed to changes and progress. Because of the complex and specialised work, they also rely heavily on education.

23 Practice passage 5

Questions, page 78

(a) (i) of their own accord and without consulting other people
 (ii) pay everything back
 (iii) evidence to show that something is true
 (iv) not being looked after properly
(b) They want the R.S.P.C.A. to help them to get their money back.
(c) This is the department which issues licences to the owners of pet-shops and could thus control what happens in the shops.
(d) increasing
(e) (The tense in the question is important. We are asked about things which the Society HAS DONE – and not about what it does or will do. We must use this tense in the answers.) Any five of the following:
 1 It has issued veterinary certificates to show the conditions of animals.
 2 It has told people to write to the Director of the Agriculture and Fisheries Department.
 3 It has told people to write to the Consumer Council.
 4 It has approached the Consumer Council.
 5 It has attended a meeting aimed at improving the situation.
 6 It has advised members not to buy animals from pet-shops which will not give customers a 'Good Health Certificate'.
 7 It has appealed to members for information and action.
(f) 1 Some of the animals are sick.
 2 The animals are overcrowded.
 3 The animals do not have adequate freedom because the cages are too small.
 4 The animals are neglected.
 5 Some animals are mistreated.
(g) It was a request that pet-shops should issue a 'Good Health Certificate' and agree to refund money if an animal became sick or died within an agreed period.
(h) They agreed but had not yet started to issue the certificates.
(i) Many customers might refuse to buy animals from them.
(j) draft answer:
 At the meeting on 20 November, the owners of pet shops met representatives from the R.S.P.C.A., the Consumer Council and the Agricultural and Fisheries Department. Complaints were made about the conditions of some animals. Cases of sick or dying animals were mentioned. The owners were told that customers wanted their money refunded.

The pet shop owners agreed that in future they would issue 'Good Health Certificates', and that they would refund money if an animal became ill or died within an agreed period.

(This contains 81 words and can be left as the final answer.)

24 Practice passage 6

Questions, page 80
(a) He has a poor opinion of such a man and implies that he is not telling the truth.
(b) (There are alternative answers.)
'drive out fear and develop confidence'
'Personally I love doing dangerous things.'
'experiencing fear and learning to overcome'
(c) He was giving a talk (line 14) on the radio.
(d) The enemy was his nervousness at speaking on the radio.
(e) Similarly ... once again I was waiting for the red light to go green.
(f) The main cause of fear was worrying about what might happen.
(g) The route round the coast was blocked by a headland, so he was forced to go on the sea-ice to get round it.
(h) It helped him to face danger and to know what to do about it.
(i)   (i) the amount a person has
    (ii) when I look back at past events
    (iii) risk of danger
    (iv) the danger caused by enemy soldiers themselves
    (v) strangely
(j) Any six from:
   1 climbing a difficult mountain
   2 on patrol behind the enemy's lines
   3 giving a talk on the radio
   4 waiting to parachute from an aeroplane
   5 being stranded on sea-ice
   6 in a modern battle
   7 during an air-raid
(k) (The answer depends upon the individual student. Students can first write in note-form the three incidents they are going to write about. Then they can use about 3–4 lines for each situation.)

25 Practice passage 7

Questions page 82
(a) To a considerable extent it does not contain the right proportions of food needed for good health.
(b) They do not understand the value of proteins.
(c) The circle starts and finishes with a bad situation.
(d) 1 underfed or ill-fed
   2 not enough strength
   3 weakened, lack energy
   4 can't work well
   5 agricultural production suffers
   6 inadequate production, underfed

15

(e) The increase in population is greater than food production can cope with.
(f) 1 Poor countries cannot afford to buy the surplus food.
2 The surplus food is not the type which is required in a particular country.
3 The surplus food is not always the type which people are accustomed to in another country, so they may not like to eat it.
(g) It is a country where agricultural production is high, and is thus a model for other countries to try to follow.
(h) Many people already suffer from malnutrition. The problem is becoming worse because of the increase in population.
(i) (i) caused by
(ii) very seriously
(iii) final
(iv) made worse
(v) people in future years
(j) begging earnestly
(k) (The key words are *causes* and *effects of malnutrition*.)

draft summary:
Sometimes malnutrition is caused by ignorance of the value of proteins. This leads to seriously unbalanced diets and to badly prepared food. As a result, the people suffer from disease, lack energy and cannot make the fullest use of the land. Agricultural production is low and there is not enough food, especially if the population is increasing. At the same time, some countries are too poor to buy surplus food (and their people do not like it).

(76 words, so this can be the final summary. It could be improved but I assume that time is short for most candidates.)

26 Practice passage 8

Questions, page 85
(a) They were laying a telephone cable across the Atlantic.
(b) It was the supply of oxygen (mentioned in line 67).
(c) 1 Their supply of oxygen would last for only three days.
2 The submarine was at a depth which made rescue very difficult.
3 It might be impossible for a rescue submarine to locate the *Pisces III* in the black depths of the ocean.
4 The site was 100 miles from Ireland and it was most difficult to get suitable rescue vessels to the site in time.
(Any three of the above reasons.)
(d) No submarine had ever been rescued from that depth before, and there were very few submersibles capable of descending 500 metres before the men's supply of oxygen gave out.
(e) The first time, the *Pisces II* could not find the *Pisces III* and had to return to the surface because of a leak. The second time, it went down again and found the *Pisces III*.
(f) *Pisces II* was manned but there was nobody inside CURV, which was directed from a surface ship.
(g) *Pisces III* sank to a depth at which frogmen could not operate.
(h) (i) extremely small
(ii) pass messages to and receive messages from
(iii) pleased and made less worried
(iv) fasten
(v) slightly

27 Practice passages 9 and 10

Passage 9, questions page 87

1   We are told that the only meat they had was roasted pigskin, so they clearly did not eat much meat.
2   She told him to take the smaller piece of bread from the bin but not to eat it until he was on his return journey.
3   The extreme cold went through the storyteller's clothes and produced pain in various parts of his body, so he felt sick. He was desperate to complete the journey and get the crackling.
4   intending to do evil
5   We are told that the children's hunger was sometimes satisfied and could be endured but that the pain and danger from the cold were much more severe.
6   He did not wait because he felt humiliated by the man and wanted to escape from his mocking stare.
7   He wanted to emphasize the fact that Aunt Liza had to do a great deal of washing. (The examiners wrote: "Most candidates misinterpreted the question to be 'Why were her hands swollen?' and mentioned that they were cold or in the washing. For this it was fair to give one mark (out of the two available). The more perceptive ones said that the author wanted to show that she had to work hard habitually, and were given full marks. Weaker candidates merely cued the sentence in the passage and said that she shook the soapsuds off her hands. This shows clearly the range of the candidates' thinking from total misunderstanding to going one step beyond what they have been told."
8   (a) The use of 'half-human monster' personifies the cold and increases its malevolence. Perhaps the children really did believe that the cold came from some type of evil force.
    (b) The cold and the monster were similar in that neither showed any pity or mercy; they were also similar in their power to inflict pain on the children.

The examiners said, "This was difficult and few answers identified the use of personification with the author's wish to emphasize the power of the cold, although many were able to compare the half-human desires to cause harm to others with the effects of the cold. It enjoyed making the children suffer, is an example of the several correct answers available."

9   The man probably thought that he was superior because he was white, because of his social standing and because he was an adult speaking to a child.

The examiners said, "This was less difficult and many candidates were able to think beyond the passage to the white man's wish to humiliate the boy and show superiority. Candidates who did not think, repeated parts of the extract or said that he had not heard the boy."

10 The passage is taken from a book, so we may guess that the author has several reasons for describing this incident. He probably resented the racism involved and the ill-treatment (by an adult) of young children. He recalled and disliked the bitter cold and the grim conditions under which he and his friends lived. We can guess that one aim of the book was to highlight the inhuman conditions under which young black children lived when he was a child and perhaps lived when he was writing his book.

The examiners said, "Candidates should be taught that in the last question (for which 5 marks were available) the number of marks is related to the number of answers given. In fact there were many points to be made, related to the theme of racism, the hardships endured by the boys, and the desire to remember and set down his own youth. Candidates were often satisfied with one point, sometimes quite repetitively extended.

This section (1–10) was frequently found to be difficult, and few scripts contained high scoring answers from beginning to end."

Passage 10, questions page 89

1 He did this because he was so frightened at first that he temporarily went to pieces and did not know what to do.
2 At first, he did not eat anything except when hunger forced him to look for something. Then he just ate boiled shellfish.
3 He decided to sleep at night (instead of watching for a ship) and searched for a place in which to sleep.
4 It is described as mean because Alex was already in a very weak mental and physical state, and the noise from the valley kept on waking him up.
5 He means that Alex was afraid that the island would be barren and inhospitable.
6 I think he felt astonished and delighted. He probably felt astonished because he had not expected to find such a pleasant and productive place. He felt delighted because he saw that the valley would produce timber, food and water for him.
7 He did not explore the valley behind Cumberland Bay despite an assurance that there was plenty of food there. Instead, he lived on an unpleasant diet of shellfish. He made no proper arrangements for regular sleep and even tried to stay awake at night. He risked his health by sitting and staring at the horizon by day and by night. The examiners said, "This is not difficult and the answers were related to eating, sleeping and watching aimlessly. A number of candidates copied chunks from the text and missed the point about not sleeping. They should have worked out the answers in their own minds first and then expressed them briefly in their own words."
8 Sandalwood provided Alex with building timber, fuel and (when burnt) a source of light at night. Watercress, turnips and cabbage palms gave him a better and more pleasant diet because they provided food.
9 Alex was pleasantly surprised to find that the climate of the valley was comparatively mild, thanks to the shelter provided by the volcanic cliffs. This made living conditions more acceptable. In addition, he found vines (for holding things together) and colourful flowers.
10 (We cannot tell from the extract where the island is, so we must invent a location. We have to give information about the three points mentioned in the question.)

HELP! Please send help! I am marooned on a small rocky island about 500 miles west of Valparaiso. I think its name is San Juan Fernandez. Conditions are terrible here. I exist on shellfish and am weak from lack of food and sleep. I am confused but pray daily for safe delivery from death by starvation. If you cannot help me yourself, please pass this to the nearest British authority. PLEASE HELP ME. Without your help, I'll surely die. Alex Selkirk

28 Practice passage 11

Questions, page 92

(a) He thought that he ought not to shoot the elephant because it was a trained, working elephant and therefore valuable to somebody. He decided that he would have to shoot the elephant because it had turned savage in the past and a huge crowd of people expected him to do this duty and shoot it.
(b) Two relevant expressions are:

    a   He looked suddenly stricken shrunken, immensely old …
    b   An enormous senility seemed to have settled upon him …
    But please note that these were NOT the effects of the "final" shot. We do not know what effects the final shot (line 52) had on the elephant. Should 'final' read 'first'?

(c) The author could not bear to watch the elephant dying, so he sent back for his small rifle, hoping to be able to put the animal out of its distress. When further shots did not kill the elephant, the author could not stand the sight any more, so he went away.

Questions, page 93

(d) He has been appointed to protect wildlife (and especially elephants and rhinos) by reducing or stopping poaching.
(e) In their struggle to stop poaching, rangers now have a most potent weapon: the right to shoot poachers with the intention of killing them. This new measure has been brought in to put down the poachers but there is considerable argument about this new (ruthless) policy.
(f) It is necessary to cull entire families of elephant so that baby elephants will not be left without a mother or protector, and so that older elephants will not suffer from shock or distress when other members of their family are killed.
(g) The slaughter of elephants has been caused by unsatisfactory treatment of park employees, the increasing value of and demand for ivory, and the work of poachers.

Questions, page 95

(h) Four of the following:
    1   The ban will alert people to the threat to elephants.
    2   It will make people avoid buying ivory products.
    3   It will lead African shops to use camel bone instead of ivory when making and selling artefacts.
    4   It will lead to a fall in the price of ivory, and thus to a decline in poaching.
    5   It will create difficulties for people trying to sell existing stocks of tusks.
(i) Some countries think that the ban will do more harm than good as far as elephants are concerned. If elephants are of no financial benefit, people may slaughter them. Zimbabwe claims that a controlled programme of culling and of stamping out poaching will be more beneficial to elephants.
(j)   (i)   when a bullet hits its target
       (ii) Inverted commas are used because the words 'shoot to kill' are a short and commonly used way of describing a particular policy, and act as a compound adjective here.
       (iii) The expression means that ivory will soon become unwanted, just as people no longer want coats made of leopard skin or handbags made from the skin of crocodiles.

29 Practice passage 12

Questions, page 98

(a) If there are sufficient trees, they deflect sound waves and thus reduce the noise made by vehicles using a road.
(b) Reasons for the loss of trees include the following:
    1   They are cut down for agriculture and grazing.
    2   They are cut down to get land for human settlement.

         3   They die through old age.
         4   They are killed by disease.
         5   They die as a result of dry land.
         6   They are killed by salinity caused by irrigation schemes.
         7   They are killed by erosion.
         8   They are destroyed by natural and man-made fires.
    (Any seven of the above reasons.)
(c) The four main causes of excess salinity on the land are said to be:
    1   When trees are cut down the water table rises, bringing salinity to the surface.
    2   Salinity is also caused by certain types of irrigation projects.
    3   This may involve inadequate drainage, another cause of salinity.
    4   In addition, the excessive use of fertilisers can increase salinity in the soil.

Questions, page 100
(d) This means that tracks which should be covered with snow (for skiing) are green with grass because no snow has fallen.
(e) Seven similarities are:
    1   Both areas are affected by pollution.
    2   Both are wilderness areas.
    3   Heavily populated regions surround them both.
    4   Although they were thought to be inexhaustible, they are highly vulnerable ecologically.
    5   Trade routes cross them.
    6   Their natural resources are harvested.
    7   Tourists flock to enjoy their beauty.
(f) The expression means "wanting to create a more favourable impression on the public as far as support for the environment is concerned".

Questions, page 101
(g) The legend about the baobab tree has evolved because of the amount of activity in the tree at night, when bats, bush babies (at dusk) and probably other creatures move about in the tree.
(h) Propagation may depend on digestion of acacia seeds by elephants. Alternatively, propagation may depend more on dropping seeds in places with enough light for growth. (25 words)

30 Practice passage 13

Questions, page 103
1   (a) yearly movement (to the island)
     (b) arrive
     (c) attraction for visitors
2   They go the wrong way because they are attracted by the lights of hotels and discotheques.
3   If tourists show that they are visiting the island to see the turtles, they may encourage the authorities to protect the turtles to safeguard the tourist trade.

Questions, page 105
4   Wolves and dogs have a very similar physique and highly developed senses, especially those of hearing, sight and smell. Both animals bark to defend their territory.

     Dogs differ from wolves in various ways. They hold their tail erect or in a curled position. Their colour patterns are now different from that of wolves. They differ also in that they are domesticated and can act as herders, whereas wolves are wild animals that live by hunting.

5   The fact that human beings were able to domesticate dogs perhaps led them to consider (and then carry out) the domestication of animals such as cattle and sheep. The author makes this suggestion because it may show how the domestication of dogs led to the discovery of agriculture.

Questions, page 106

6   (a) He crushed his watch to show that he had broken with modern living and was going to rely on nature (to tell him the time).
    (b) He mentions the boys to show the serenity of life some time ago, before the town was affected by modern technology.
    (c) The whaling industry is an example of something which, with the aid of modern technology, may have a disastrous effect on whales and thus on nature.

7   (a) The use of 'the summer' would suggest a reference to a single year but the use of 'a summer' suggests that the turtles lay nests every year.
    (b) We could use a full stop instead of the semicolon.
    (c) living in packs
    (d) He uses 'i.e.' to show that an explanation follows.
    (e) The use of 'still' stresses the fact that large numbers of whales existed despite the fact that they had been hunted extensively.
    (f) With his technical progress, man could one day bring an end to nature's eternal supply of whales.

31 Practice passage 14

Please note that the 'Comments' after the suggested answers are taken from the Examiners' Report on the examination.

Questions, page 107

1   (a) It tells us that he tried very hard but failed (to lever up the island).
    (b) It tells us that Easter Island was made of extremely hard rock.

Comments: The opening questions, Qs 1 and 2, were basically a series of factual tests, calling for isolation of appropriate text evidence. Candidates could earn marks simply by reproducing the text as it stood, or by paraphrasing it. However, there were many answers which were unnecessarily prolix, and it seemed that the effort to write at length caused candidates to lose sight of the required essence of the answer. Thus, in handling the simple opening tests of Qs 1(a) and 1(b), some were too keen to write about the whole activity of the giant, and thus failed to select the two straightforward elements required as answers, i.e. the giant's failure to lever up the island, and its rocky nature.

2   (a) It tells us that Easter Island is in the Pacific Ocean and is probably the only island in the area because the giant removed all the others.
    (b) (i) with people living (there)
        (ii) almost completely
    (c) He wants us to understand that the 'hotel' is of a low standard.
    (d) In the earlier years of this century, a hotel was unnecessary because it was impossible to reach the island except on a ship which called once a year. Any visitor would have to stay at least a year and would seek accommodation other than that provided by a normal hotel.
    (e) A hotel has become necessary because there is an airport, so more visitors can reach the island. They will need somewhere to stay.

Comments: Fluent, accurate English often characterised writing throughout the paper, even where marks were lost for misjudging the aim of the question. In itself, this command of English enabled candidates to score marks in tackling the purely linguistic tests such as question 2(b)(i), with only the weaker ones being influenced by 'remote', close to the question word 'inhabited'; they made the false assumption that nobody lived there. The trickier idiom of question 2(b)(ii) produced some brave attempts, and even if the simple equivalents like 'almost' or 'very nearly' were missed, the closeness of the answers showed that candidates were thinking along the right lines. The mistake here was to wander off into a protracted account of the inaccessibility of the island, which was in itself no answer to the linguistic test involved.

Question 2(c) again required some appreciation of mature English idiom, and there were some good answers here, demonstrating that fluency of English already referred to, with apposite expressions such as 'a make-shift hotel' or 'a hotel without the usual amenities'. Those who misjudged the test of the question wrote at length about the non-existence of hotels of any type on the island. Overall, the greatest success in this part of the paper came from answers to questions 2(d) and 2(c). The majority of scripts scored at least one mark in question 2(d) for correctly interpreting lines 10–15, noting either the difficulty of access to the island or the infrequency of contact. The second mark needed the inference drawn from the infrequency of contact that there were few visitors, and the correct answers here showed that some candidates were alert to this particular type of test. The same candidates also handled question 2(e) successfully, producing once again comprehensive and fluent writing about the presence of an airport and the resulting increase in visitors.

Questions, page 108

3   He wanted to be physically closer to them, e.g. by visiting the island and standing by the figures.

Comments: A number of answers to question 3 showed a secure grasp of idiom and understanding, with encouraging responses such as 'the author wanted to see the statues face to face' or 'the author wanted to see the statues in real life'. The weak responses misjudged the reference of the phrase being tested and talked instead of the author wanting to explore the island or of getting to know its culture. In fact, the frequency of misaligned answers increased as the paper developed, and it seemed that candidates were unable to maintain techniques of aligning question material to textual evidence, or of considering the rubric carefully before beginning to write anything down.

Questions, page 109

4   (a) He expected to see hungry people because there was very little land on the island suitable for growing crops or for raising cattle.
    (b) Normally 'logs' is used to refer to timber; in addition, we would not expect to see huge pieces of rock that are long and thin.
    (c) This means large pieces of stone which were nearly fully formed, partly formed or hardly formed at all – showing a range of work on the figures.

Comments: Thus, the 'own words' prescript of question 4(a) was often ignored, and answers relying on verbatim text lifts such as 'the land was barren and would not support crops' appeared in many scripts. Perhaps some candidates felt that they were at liberty to use the text, provided that they set it in a sentence of their own composition, and indeed a number of answers were seen of some length, but with the core entirely dependent on the text. What in fact candidates had to do was to analyse lines 26–28 and select the elements they thought relevant to the answer, and then re-phrase those elements in their own language. Some correct answers were seen, e.g. 'the soil was infertile' or 'there was hardly any productive soil', but they were in the minority.

Question 4(c) set a similar test, but once again the relevant area of the text had to be examined to see the reference of the phrase being tested. Lines 35–38, with the details of 'fully formed statues' and 'huge, unshaped 'logs' of rock', point to the range of complete and incomplete carvings, the context that was linked to the question wording 'every stage between'. A hurried reading of the question produced many literal interpretations, e.g. that there were carved figures lying between the rocks or that there were figures of different shapes and sizes lying everywhere. Question 4(b) was not such a sophisticated test or text reference – it only required that the answer refer to what was 'unusual' about using 'logs' to describe rock. Those who kept the focus of the question in view had no difficulty here; they answered simply, but correctly, that 'logs' usually refer to timber or wood, not stone, or that rocks are not usually long in shape like logs. The hasty answer concentrated instead on descriptions of the 'logs' of rock, namely that they were long and round, or that they were lying around like logs, omitting any reference to what was 'unusual' about the descriptions.

Questions, page 110

5 (a) He thought that if the statues could talk, they would say who the carvers were.
(b) The dates are surprising because of the wide range between the 7th and the 16th centuries. The author probably expected experts to be more precise with the date.
(c) Scholars have tried to learn the language used by the carvers (which would contain information about the islanders). Their failure to decipher the signs is unexpected because scholars have studied them for many years and there are many inscriptions available for study.

Comments: The same sort of inability to fasten on the aim of the question and examine the text carefully led to a sad loss of marks by many candidates in question 5(a). They only needed to align the question with lines 65–66 to see that the author would have known who the carvers were, if the statues could have talked. Instead, the frequent answers were that he would have known who they were, which left the examiner to relate 'they' to the implied antecedent of the question wording, i.e. the statues, or even that the author would have known who the statues were, which shows a very swift reading of the text evidence. Some answers merely re-stated the question wording, e.g. 'they appeared like humans, just ready to talk', betraying a poor understanding of how to set about answering what after all was a fairly typical test of text comprehension.

The candidates, on the other hand, who carefully weighed up the wording of questions 5(b) and 5(c) scored at least two of the four marks available. In question 5(b) it was important to see that the 'surprising' nature of the dates needed the comment, i.e. that they were too wide or vague, coming from so-called experts. Answers that commented in general terms about the dates, e.g. that the carvers arrived a long time ago, or that they could never have worked when they did because there were not tools for carving, had clearly missed the force of 'surprising' in the question wording.

Question 5(c) maintained the purely factual level of testing and required a division of response, i.e. to state what the scholars tried to learn and why their failure was 'unexpected'. Once more, there was a marked difference of approach here. The candidates who had observed the rubric marshalled the evidence of the text accordingly, from lines 74–76, with many of them correctly stating that scholars had tried to decipher the inscriptions and then had failed, despite many years of study, so gaining two out of the three marks available. Close attention to the text was required to earn the third mark, for noting that the number of inscriptions to be found also made the failure 'unexpected'.

Answers like these showed a proper technique, in contrast to those which bore no relation to the text evidence and commented instead on the difficulty of carving with a stone tool or on the abandonment of statues. Somehow, 'failure' was linked with the original carving of the statues and related to text a long way from paragraph 8. Candidates are always given help in the question headings; they direct the candidates to the area of search, but clearly even this basic direction was ignored by some of them.

Questions, page 110

6 (a) (i) The islanders might have been attacked (and killed ?) by strangers who managed to reach the island; this would have caused work on the carving to stop.
      (ii) Perhaps the islanders thought they saw a ghost and this caused them to stop work on the statues.
      (iii) Perhaps something caused widespread panic on the island, and this led to a cessation of the carving.
      (iv) Perhaps fighting broke out amongst the islanders and all energies were turned towards settling the dispute.
  (b) The giant tried hard to lever up Easter Island. Similarly, the experts tried hard to decipher the inscriptions. Both failed in their tasks.

Comments: In question 6(a) a correct understanding of the rubric was essential if any sensible answers were to be offered. Simple statements had to be written, re-setting the four words or phrases as reasons for the destruction of the statues. As in previous questions, the relevant area of the text had to be located in order to see the aim of the question, and lines 83–84 gave the lead there. It was only those candidates who studied this context who produced satisfactory 'reasons', chiefly for (i) 'invasion' and (iv) 'civil strife'. Others, however, either wrote single word answers, despite the rubric instruction calling for sentences, or ignored the context of the question altogether, and rehashed lines 77–82, describing the destruction and abandonment of the statues, without attempting any reasons. Many who either had not offered any response at all to question 6(a), or whose answers indicated a serious misunderstanding of its instructions, recovered to some extent in tackling question 6(b). The question required a comparison of the paragraphs 1 and 8 to arrive at the point of similarity in the experience of the giant and scholars. Those who made the comparison often provided one element of similarity, i.e. their common failure. The second point of similarity, that both expended a great deal of effort, needed closer scrutiny of the two paragraphs; the more observant candidates managed to isolate it. A number of answers mistakenly assigned the same area of failure to the giant and scholars alike, claiming that both had failed to destroy or lever up the island. This mistake showed a narrow concentration on the first paragraph, despite the fact that the scholars did not appear there.

Question, page 111

7 1 whole
    2 anxious (enthusiastic; very willing)
    3 extremely surprising (astonishing)
    4 obvious (clear)
    5 hardly (almost not)
    6 gathering (grouping)
    7 puzzled
    8 inferred (concluded)

Comments: Question 7, with its straightforward test of word substitution, produced a rather meagre average of marks on the majority of scripts. It was clear from the answers on many scripts that the words in some cases had not been set in text to see their usage, and inappropriate dictionary definitions were substituted, such as 'sharp' for 'keen' or 'thinking deeply' for 'concentration'. Candidates should note the rubric in this question, that the equivalent offered should have the same meaning as the original word has in the passage. If this rubric is observed at the outset, then candidates will give themselves a better chance of selecting the correct application of a word, and will avoid offering the totally incorrect alternative. At the same time, the force of words should be considered in context. 'Astounding', in line 20, closely aligned to 'gigantic', meant that the figures were more than 'surprising', one of the common, but incorrect answers. 'Scarcely' also proved difficult to re-set if its adverbial usage had not been seen in line 27. Words or phrases stating quantity, such as 'small amount' or 'very little', were common attempts, but just would not fit into the passage. Nor should candidates offer derivatives of the word being tested, such as 'it appears' for 'apparent'; no marks can ever be earnt adopting that technique. The range of answers overall suggests that a sharper awareness of what words are doing in context would have guided candidates' thinking and given them a better chance to display their knowledge of vocabulary.

32 Practice passage 15

Questions, page 113
1. satanic atmosphere (witches' cauldron)
2. cooking pot
3. It did not melt in the hot sun. (It prevented water from entering a ship.)
4. dull
5. (One of:) one must keep driving
   frequently develops a soft spot
   a treacherous black treacle
6. marvel
7. a skeleton (wood 5000 years old)
8. It tells us that the Lake is probably at least 5000 years old.
9. They have been studying it since the 18th century, i.e. for at least 200 years.
10. The Man in the Lake.
11. The only reason specifically mentioned in the passage is the first one below, so presumably we have to infer or guess other reasons. If that is so, we can use any three of these reasons:
    1. A large quantity of asphalt is exported for use in road construction.
    2. Perhaps pitch is still exported for use in sailing ships.
    3. It is an interesting puzzle for scientists.
    4. It is probably a tourist attraction.
    5. It is a danger to nearby buildings and to local people.
12. (a) oozes – turns into something like a liquid
        treacle – a thick, semi-liquid, substance
    (b) pulled by a force from below
    (c) extremely unusual natural event
13. They have studied how the Lake came to exist in the first place, how it was formed and what is in and below it.
14. According to legend, the Lake was created as an act of revenge. Some Chayama Indians killed sacred Humming Birds in which ancestral souls were believed to live. The Carib Gods punished the Indians by turning the area into 'bubbling tar under which everything sank forever'.
15. When the words of the calypso were written down and read, they lacked music and the voice of the singer, so they had less appeal.

33 Practice passage 16

Questions, page 117
1. To become a nurse.
2. It was too short and lumpy.

25

3 boisterous
4 somebody driving sheep to pasture
5 her parents and members of her family
6 four
7 separate
8 An obeah woman had done something to them – perhaps sprinkled something on them.
9 ill-feeling
10 They were shocked by Annie's rebelliousness.
11   (i) From the three things, we learn that Annie won prizes at school, received gifts from her mother, sometimes visited the sea and wore special shoes on Sundays.
  (ii) The first of the two sentences gives us the impression that Annie was very happy at home. However, this view is contradicted in the second sentence, in which Annie says she is delighted at the thought of not seeing her home again.
12 We know (from paragraph 3) that Annie had already resolved not to marry, and most certainly not to marry an old man like her father. Hence the idea of marriage seemed absurd to Annie.
13 Whatever might happen, there was only one course of action I would follow.
14 One example of Annie's hypocrisy is the way in which she had arranged to leave home permanently without letting her parents know. Annie thought that she had been fooled when her mother had said that she could not live without her but had several times proposed ways of getting rid of Annie.
15 It was a special Sunday dinner (although it was not a Sunday), complete with special bread. The family had not been to church before the meal, and they had breakfast at a later time than on normal weekdays.

34 Practice passage 17

Questions, page 118

1   (a) The doctors resented Miss Nightingale because she was being sent to them by the Government (whether they liked it or not), she was a young lady – presumably inexperienced – from the upper class, and the doctors did not think that nursing soldiers was a suitable occupation for women.
  (b) The doctors had a poor opinion of the Government because they referred to 'Government foolishness'.
  (c) Miss Nightingale was known to have powerful support from within the Government, so anybody who opposed her openly would be in trouble with Government officials.
  (d) This means that had a different opinion from that of others.

Questions, page 119

2   (a) It tells me that the flattering attention was feigned and not genuine.
  (b) Their quarters were so bad that they soon realised that they were not really welcome and that they had been deceived.
  (c) They would be warned not to believe promises made to them, especially those made by officials in England.
3   (a) They could remember that the wounded soldiers had to endure much worse conditions than anything they had to face. This made their own problems seem less harsh.
  (b) This means that morale fell amongst the nurses and they all felt depressed.

Questions, page 120

4   They felt that if they accepted help from Miss Nightingale, they would be admitting that the army was unable to cope with the situation without help. In addition, the doctors felt that, if they accepted help, they would be penalised by their superiors later on.
5   The nurses disagreed with Miss Nightingale's actions because they did not like to stand aside when wounded men needed help, and because they had come to the Crimea to nurse men and not to count and mend linen.
6   Although there was food, it could not be cooked properly, so it was 'almost uneatable'. When given to sick patients, it merely made their condition worse. Thus the patients were starving because there was nothing fit for them to eat.

Questions, page 121

7   (a) A crisis arose when a large (and unexpected) number of wounded men arrived and the army medical staff could not deal with them without the help of Miss Nightingale and her nurses.
    (b) 1 Without the female nurses, the dressings on some of the wounded men could not be changed.
        2 Wounded men had to lie on dirty floors because there were not enough beds.
        3 Rats ran amongst the 'beds' in the wards and corridors.
    (c) In 1854, surgeons did not have the anaesthetics and equipment which reduce or suppress the pain in modern operations. At that time, operations were carried out without any effective anaesthetic, so they were much more painful.
8   (a) Although she had supplies, she did not issue them on her own initiative. She waited until a medical officer asked for them, thus leaving the initiative with the army doctors.
    (b) It means 'step by step' or 'as time passed'.

Questions, page 122

9   1 give in (to what the Government had decided to do)
    2 extremely unpleasant to carry out
    3 the place where the nurses had to live
    4 show (by her actions)
    5 unavoidably
    6 add to
    7 fated (or inevitably forced)
    8 feelings and thoughts

35 Understanding situations

Exercise 1, page 124

1   (a) She will resent the remark and feel that it is unsympathetic.
    (b) She will be pleased at the kindness shown to her.
2   (a) She might admire the hat and want to find out where to get a similar one.
    (b) She might think that the hat is weird or very unsuitable.
3   (i)   I was sorry to hear that your mother passed away.
    (ii) Excuse me, Sir, can you please help me?
    (iii) I'm afraid you've dialled a wrong number.
    (iv) I would love to come, but I'm not feeling well.

Exercise 2, page 125

1. (a) This shows that my father is sympathetic and understanding. (It could also show that he is not interested in me.)
   (b) This would show a callous and uncaring attitude.
2. (a) This shows that the driver is courteous.
   (b) This shows rudeness and hostility.
3. (a) He will resent this remark and cease to be a friend.
   (b) He will be pleased that I followed up his recommendation.
4. (a) He might think that the T-shirt is not worth $35, so he will be angry.
   (b) He might resent the fact that I have told him about the purchase.
5. (a) I think he is an unhelpful and bad salesman who is unlikely to do well.
   (b) I think he is helpful and good at his business. He will sell many shoes with this attitude.

Exercise 3, page 126

1. (a) This shows that he is being sarcastic and unfriendly.
   (b) I would think that he is not sympathetic and does not really care whether I pass or not.
2. (a) My friend is pleased at my success.
   (b) I might feel that my friend is just joking. I would not be offended. I would feel sorry for my friend.
3. (a) This would show that I am rude and perhaps arrogant.
   (b) This would show that I am trying to be tactful but honest.
4. (a) She will be pleased.
   (b) She will not be happy at all.
5. (a) My friend might be trying to give an excuse which will change the teacher's attitude.
   (b) My friend may be trying to gain the sympathy of the teacher for me, so that the teacher will stop scolding.

Exercise 4, page 127

1. (a) I would think that my friend is rude and ungrateful.
   (b) I would think that my friend is being polite in a formal way. (I would expect my friend to say, "I've eaten …" and wonder why he said "I have eaten …")
2. (a) This suggests that I want to stand on my own feet but will not abandon my parents; I am grateful to them and will help when necessary.
   (b) This shows that I am ungrateful and unfilial.
3. (a) This shows a polite and sensible attitude.
   (b) This shows a discourteous or rude attitude.
4. (a) He would be annoyed with the waiter and would rebuke him.
   (b) He would probably approve of the waiter's polite attitude.
5. (a) He may be warning me because I am taking a foolish risk.
   (b) He may be feeling resigned and be making what he thinks is a prophecy.

Part 3: Communication in writing: composition

36 Communication in writing

Exercise 1, page 132
Probable tenses are:
1. Simple Future
2. Past, Present, Future
3. Past, Present, Future
4. Past and perhaps Present
5. Conditional
6. Past
7. Past, Present and Future
8. Present and Conditional

Exercise 2, page 133
This depends on the candidate but possible answers are:

1, 2, 4, 6, 7, 8, 9, 10

Exercise 3, page 134
1. A – irrelevant
   B – irrelevant
   C – irrelevant
   D – suitable
   E – suitable
2. A, B and C are all irrelevant and unsuitable.
3. B and C are reasonable. A and D are not.
4. C is the only relevant theme.
5. A – wrong because it deals with only one custom.
   B – irrelevant
   C – may be relevant or irrelevant, depending on how it is tackled.
   D – suitable
   E – quite unsuitable
6. A – this might be relevant, depending on what 'use' means to the writer.
   B – not relevant
   C – probably relevant
   D – quite unsuitable

As an alternative or supplement to this type of exercise, we can give topics like these to students and require them to write down a topic in a single sentence.

Exercise 4, page 135
1. B is the only acceptable theme.
   C could be suitable if the writer keeps house.
2. C and D are suitable.
3. A and D are suitable.
4. A and D are suitable.
5. C is the best theme.
   A is possible.
   B is unlikely to produce a good essay.
   D and E are irrelevant.
6. C is the only suitable theme.

37 Composition – basic points

Exercise 1, page 138
1 I will describe different causes of traffic accidents and some remedies.
2 I will describe different types of films.
3 I will describe different attitudes to television.
4 I will describe different types of pollution and how we can try to reduce or eliminate them.

Exercise 2, page 140
1 I will describe the different ways in which the climate affects the people of my country.
2 I will describe some of the more common situations which lead to loneliness, and how it affects people.
3 I will describe an election.
4 I will describe a ferry, giving all the information asked for in the topic.
5 I will tell the story of an incident that changed the course of an imaginary girl's life.
6 I will describe different types of dancing and different attitudes to them.
7 I will say that both pens and shovels are useful and essential, and I will show why this is so in life.
8 I will give an account of the major events in my country last year.
9 I will describe the characteristics of a good friend.

Exercise 3, page 140
1 I will describe a visit I have made to Disneyland.
2 I will discuss the need for discipline (but not an excessive amount of it) at home and in school.
3 I will describe different types of unwelcome visitors.
4 I will discuss both sides of the statement.
5 I will describe different types of smugglers.
6 I will describe a particularly cold winter which I can remember, going from its start to the time it finished.
7 I will describe some of the things people collect and try to explain why they collect them.
8 I will explain how I have enjoyed helping people in the past, and then try to say to what extent my education will enable me to help people in the future.
9 I will discuss the major areas in which safety is a problem in the home.
10 I will write a long letter, as requested, describing my personal pleasures at home and beyond it.

41 Finishing a composition

Test page 151
1 The theme.
2 At least 15 minutes.
3 It depends upon what you are writing but 6–12 lines is reasonable in most cases.
4 This shows ways of finding a theme if one is not given.
5 (a) I will describe different types of doctors.
  (b) I will try to describe possible causes for juvenile crime and possible ways of reducing it.

6   None at all. She must describe the building and not how she reached or left it.
7   With dialogue, action or a statement of one's theme.
8   By summing up or looking into the future.
9   A dark colour – black or dark blue. It is easier to read.
10 However, there is another side to this argument.
11 6–12.
12 (a) I will describe the advantages and disadvantages of water.
    (b) I will describe the different attitudes which people have to clothes.
13 (a) Water plays a very important part in the life of all living things. It has many advantages but can produce problems.
    (b) Different people often have very different attitudes to clothes. For example, my sister spends all of her money and most of her time selecting and buying the most modern clothes.
14 Know how many words you write per line. Then count the lines.

42 What kind of English shall I use?

Exercise 1, page 155
1   The money spent on space travel could be more usefully spent on projects on Earth.
2   The Government should help to reduce accidents in the home.
3   I enjoy woodwork and find it a useful hobby.

43 Further practice with basic skills

Exercise 1, page 156
1   A and C are reasonable.
2   A – No. This is not a campaign.
    B – No, as above.
    C – No. We are not asked to deal with a country.
    D – No. We are asked how to conduct a campaign and not to give reasons for conducting it.
3   A and B are reasonable.
    C is irrelevant.
    D is probably irrelevant but could be made relevant.
4   C and D are better than A or B.
5   A – no, not both.
    B – no, not in history but in sport
    C – irrelevant
    D – irrelevant as it stands
6   A – no, not overseas
    B – no, as above
    C – reasonable
    D – the second line is wrong.
7   A – not very good; it is only one strike.
    B – quite irrelevant
    C – reasonable
    D – possible but incomplete if it deals only with the 19th century
8   A and B are reasonable.

C is factually wrong.
D – probably irrelevant because much of the composition may be about preparing and failing rather than about success. Some examiners would accept this theme; others would reject it.
9. A – just possible
   B – rather unlikely
   C and D – reasonable
10. A, C and D are reasonable
    B might be reasonable; this depends on what individual markers think.

Exercise 2, page 158

1. A, B and C are reasonable.
   D – probably satisfactory but some markers might object.
2. A and B are irrelevant.
   C and D are relevant.
3. Only A is relevant.
4. A – incomplete; no mention has been made of success.
   B, C and D are all irrelevant.
   (C does not explain why students take the examination.)
5. A, B, C and D are all relevant.
6. A, B and D are reasonable.
   C is probably too one-sided to be acceptable.
7. B, C and D are reasonable.
   A is probably too restricted in scope.
8. D is relevant.
   A, B and C are unsuitable.
9. A – unsuitable
   B – possible if cleverly done
   C – reasonable
   D – reasonable
10. C and D are relevant.
    B might be relevant, depending on what the writer says.
    A is quite irrelevant.

Exercise 3, page 160

1. I will describe the major uses of electricity.
2. I will describe the basic skills needed in photography.
3. I will describe some of the situations in which the proverb may be true.
4. I will discuss the accuracy of the judge's remark, explaining what he meant and saying whether or not he was right.
5. I will describe a time when I hurt my left leg.
6. I will try to describe the evolution and nature of bureaucracy and then glance at its future in society.
7. I will try to account for the tendency in modern times for groups of countries to form regional associations.
8. In their order of importance, I will explain the lessons which students can probably learn from History.
9. I will discuss the different attitudes which people have to charity.
10. I will describe the extent to which clothes reveal a person's character.

Part 4: Vocabulary

54 Words in context

Exercise 1, page 206
1. came suddenly to
2. plausible salesman
3. tiny
4. growing
5. stock (many valuable sites)
6. terraced
7. sound
8. well known
9. on very friendly terms
10. state
11. romantic involvement
12. make a start
13. descend
14. write down
15. annoyed
16. extinguish
17. leave outside
18. erected
19. moved up and shook
20. threw a ball

Exercise 2, page 207
1. final
   the one before us
2. Nobody has stayed long.
   There has been no manager for many months.
3. excellent
   not yet available
4. was standing beside
   continued to support
5. She can't read it.
   She can speak no other language.
6. When
   Because
7. unpunctual
   has only just come
8. very good
   bad
9. I can buy some only.
   I cannot buy any of them.
10. reduce
    write down

Exercise 3, page 208
1. a list of items; a ship develops a list before sinking
2. join a club; hit somebody with a club
3. put a bracket after a word; put a bracket under a shelf
4. will hurt if touched; an invitation to buy
5. mail; a wooden post
6. a belief; being found guilty of a crime
7. together with; against
8. not on time; dead

Exercise 4, page 208
1. victim being chased; a place where sand or stone is dug from the ground
2. comb your hair; search thoroughly
3. give money to a conqueror; praise somebody
4. rise from the ground; deduct; imitate and mock
5. not living; exactly
6. eat no food; quick(ly)
7. eventually; before an agreed time

Exercise 5, page 208
1. (a) Uncle wrote it.
   (b) It was the second book he wrote.

33

2 (a) She voted for him or abstained.
   (b) She voted against somebody else.
3 (a) ... but other things do.
   (b) You are wrong to think that they are punctual.
4 (a) It does not sell any other kind.
   (b) No other shop sells them.
5 (a) He is the best of them all.
   (b) but they can do other things as well as he can.

Exercise 6, page 209
1 suspended; not being observed or carried out
2 speeded up
3 sound qualities
4 change to meet changed conditions
5 keeping; sticking to; following
6 wealth
7 make it worse
8 having two meanings
9 facilities; attractions
10 good-natured
11 able to operate on land and on water
12 from an unknown person

55 Antonyms, synonyms and homonyms

Antonyms page 210
(a) illegal, unlawful
(b) None of the words are antonyms. 'Understood' and 'appreciated' are synonyms but we are not asked for synonyms here.

Exercise 1, page 210
1 simple
2 civilised
3 guilty
4 confident
5 against
6 refreshed (fit)
7 without
8 well-informed (sophisticated)
9 badly
10 old (well-known)

Exercise 2, page 211
1 (a) with a grudge, disgruntled, annoyed about something
   (b) not yet met or fulfilled
2 (a) find out
   (b) reveal, take off a cover
3 (a) not qualified (for a job)
   (b) prevented from taking part in something because of some fault
4 (a) take away; drive somebody out of something
   (b) claim back again
5 (a) not used before or at present
   (b) no longer fit to be used
6 (a) with bad morals
   (b) not concerned with morals

Exercise 3, page 212

1. illegible
2. improper
3. dishonourable
4. unconfirmed
5. illogical
6. irresponsible
7. indefensible
8. irrational
9. non-flammable
10. disagreement
11. anti-climax
12. misbehave

Exercise 4, page 212

1. put in
2. sedate
3. insult
4. intending to hurt
5. warned; scolded and told
6. immediately
7. daring, bold
8. thought to himself
9. risky, dangerous
10. thing which might happen
11. approaching
12. coming

Exercise 5, page 213

Various sentences are possible with these words:

1. foul
2. fort
3. steak
4. veil
5. berth
6. beach
7. meddle
8. right
9. tort
10. gait

Exercise 6, page 214

1. that which is inherited or passed from somebody to his descendants; passes on; leaves to a person on death
2. suitable
3. taken swiftly and without consulting others
4. people (often civil servants) who work in offices
   well known for their bad qualities
5. keep away from; not buy
6. disguise
7. frankness
   careful about what you say
8. thoroughtfully
   (letter) written by somebody else in an attempt to deceive
9. speech
10. taken away from them
11. incapable of being appeased or calmed down
12. tips; gifts of money

56 Pairs of words

Exercise 1, page 215

1. (a) They both imply not fat, slender.
   (b) 'Thin' can have an unfavourable connotation, implying that a person ought to be fatter. 'Slim' has a favourable connotation.
2. (a) Both are measures of length.
   (b) Yards are used in the imperial system formerly used in the U.K. and still used in parts of the U.S.A. Metres are measurements of the metric system.

3 (a) Both are measures of time.
   (b) A second is a sixtieth part of a minute. A month is a twelfth part of a year.
4 (a) Both are used to record the passing of time.
   (b) A clock records hours and minutes, whereas a calendar records days and months.
5 (a) Both can enclose a field or a house.
   (b) A fence may be man-made but a hedge is a natural formation of bushes, trees, etc.
6 (a) Both can fly.
   (b) A helicopter has a rotating wing. An aeroplane (in common usage) is a fixed-wing aircraft.
7 (a) Both show femininity.
   (b) A female is (broadly speaking) something which has the potential to become a mother; it may be a fish or a human being. A woman is an adult, female human being.
8 (a) Both bring relief to a problem.
   (b) A solution solves a problem but a cure usually cures a disease.
9 (a) Both are connected with written symbols.
   (b) A letter is a single symbol within an alphabet. An alphabet is a collection of letters. Thus 'm' is a letter and not under any circumstances an alphabet. A young child learns the alphabet (A–Z in English) or learns the separate letters of the alphabet, e.g. 's' and 't'.
10 (a) Both can carry people.
   (b) People have to pay fares on a bus, which is a form of public or private transport. A coach is usually a single-decker and is often used for carrying groups who have paid before they get on the coach.

Exercise 2, page 216
1 took
2 conscientious
3 recommend
4 take
5 hope
6 wish
7 wear
8 watch
9 attracted
10 is worth
11 hard
12 like

Exercise 3, page 217
1 while
2 robbed, took
3 pay, spend
4 initiative
5 reason
6 cause
7 bare
*8 replaced
*9 substitute
10 altogether
11 very much
12 assure

*In their active forms, 'replace' usually involves taking a person or thing out. Then 'substitute' means putting a person or thing in place of another person or thing. An injured player can be replaced. Another player will be a substitute for the injured player. Even native-speakers sometimes confuse these two words.

Exercise 4, page 218
1 D 2 A 3 B 4 B 5 C 6 B 7 A 8 B 9 D 10 B

57 Phrasal verbs

Matching exercise pages 219–220
1 e 2 m 3 h 4 b 5 g 6 f 7 j 8 o 9 a 10 l 11 d 12 k
13 n 14 c 15 i

Exercise 1, page 220

1. demolish
2. extract
3. recover/survive
4. stopped
5. cooperate
6. attract
7. obtain it/succeed
8. drive
9. overcome
10. deceive me

Exercise 2, page 221

1. propose/put forward/produce
2. postpone
3. increased/raised
4. tolerate/endure
5. save/keep
6. collided with/hit
7. tolerate/abide/accept
8. represents/means
9. avoid/escape from
10. disappointed
11. submitted/surrendered/gave up
12. delayed

Exercise 3, page 225

1. cooperate
2. submit/make
3. applied
4. delayed
5. interrupted
6. cancelled/abandoned
7. revive
8. visit
9. cancel/postpone/abandon
10. met
11. abandon
12. kill/murder
13. criticising
14. pass
15. organise/obtain/collect
16. made/signed/finalised
17. precipitated/produced/led to/caused
18. tolerate/endure/accept/permit
19. found
20. obtain/get

Exercise 4, page 228

1. deceived
2. investigate
3. be in charge of
4. like
5. make a habit of
6. met by chance
7. endure/have
8. maintain the same standard of living
9. released
10. looks (and perhaps acts) like
11. supported/remained with
12. imitate
13. scorn/despise
14. started/began/commenced
15. mentioned (perhaps superficially)

Exercise 5, page 229

1. get on
2. get up
3. get through
4. get away
5. get back
6. get out of
7. get in(to)
8. get off
9. get up
10. get over

Exercise 6, page 230

1. making for
2. make up
3. make up
4. make out
5. make for
6. make off

Exercise 7, page 230

1. lay down, give up
2. pull down, knock down
3. put off
4. bring up
5. came across, bumped into
6. given up
7. look into
8. looked through, went through
9. back you up, stand by
10. turned down
11. taking out
12. look up to, think highly of

37

58 Prefixes and meaning

Exercise 1, page 232

1. (a) across, (b) across the Pacific Ocean
2. (a) before, (b) to date something earlier than the day on which the decision is made
3. (a) against, (b) against a revolution (but the term has conveniently different uses in different countries)
4. (a) former, (b) the person who was once chairman
5. (a) self, (b) the story of a person's life, written by himself
6. (a) two, (b) having two meanings
7. (a) below, (b) below normal levels
8. (a) below, inadequately, b inadequately nourished, with insufficient food
9. (a) after, (b) treatment or something else after the birth of a child
10. (a) beyond, outside, (b) classes given 'outside the walls' of a college or university – usually for ordinary members of the public
11. (a) one, (b) in one tone, boring
12. (a) life, (b) a person who studies living things

Exercise 2, page 233

1. (a) away from (b) not present
2. (a) chief (b) a chief angel
3. (a) well (b) meaning or wishing well, acting in a kindly way
4. (a) across (b) the distance from one side to another, measured through the centre
5. (a) far, a long distance (b) a message sent quickly, often from a distance
6. (a) against (b) to hold back, not to give
7. (a) life (b) a person who studies the chemistry of living things
8. (a) around (b) to sail or go round the world
9. (a) with (b) to work on friendly terms with
10. (a) equal (b) of equal distance
11. (a) many (b) having many spouses
12. (a) eight (b) a marine animal with eight legs

Exercise 3, page 233

1. labour, labourer
2. library, librarian
3. inhabit, inhabitant
4. magnify, magnitude
5. convert, revert, subvert
6. agriculture
7. manual
8. manufacture
9. annual
10. navigation

Exercise 4, page 234

1. contraband, contradict
2. contradict, dictation, edict, indict
3. cubicle
4. feminine, effeminate
5. expect, expectations
6. occupy, occupant
7. marine, mariner, submarine
8. miser, miserable, misery
9. September (which was once the seventh month of the year)
10. satisfactory, satisfaction

Exercise 5, page 234

1. an elephant
2. a barbarian
3. Britain
4. a captive
5. I confirm
6. I defend

7 I despair
8 difficult
9 I exclaim
10 I expel
11 a flame

12 Germans
13 honesty
14 a doctor
15 I recite

59 Problem words and correct usage 1

Exercise 1, page 235
1 boring, bored
2 boring
3 boring
4 excited

5 excited
6 exciting
7 frustrated
8 frustrating, frustrated

Exercise 2, page 236
1 difference
2 difference
3 different
4 difference

5 silent
6 Silence
7 silent
8 silence

60 Problem words and correct usage 2

Exercise 1, page 240
1 very annoying
2 all disgusted
3 much difference
4 of patience
5 to practise
6 The number
7 There are
8 was dead
9 the furniture
10 the apparatus

11 of fun
12 much effect
13 of homework
14 to raise
15 ran past
16 seriously injured
17 Is anybody
18 my belongings
19 other words
20 the young

Exercise 2, page 245
1 is falling
2 difficult words
3 (Omit 'by heart'.)
4 dead on time
5 a lot of damage
6 become unemployed
7 very tired
8 even if they have
9 very grateful
10 no matter whether

11 accompanied me
12 a neglect of
13 because there was not enough time
14 all the shouting *or* all the shouts
15 underlying causes
16 Faced with
17 will not let me watch
18 I very much agree with
19 letter in today's newspaper
20 as time passed

Exercise 3, page 246
1 very astonished and almost unable to speak
2 any unpleasant occurrence
3 with its front part rising and falling in the sea

4 wicked, evil
5 boring
6 persistently (despite the bad conditions); in a determined manner
7 type (of fish)
8 cracks in rocks
9 home and hiding-place; get it out
10 a great deal; freely
11 aggressive attitude; impressed and slightly frightened
12 liable to be affected; people who deliberately start a fire
13 watchful, on guard; question
14 permit; main
15 given unfavourable treatment

6 | Idioms and common expressions

Exercise 1, page 247
1 fear (or pleasurable anticipation)
2 anger or determination
3 bewilderment or uncertainty
4 surprise or doubt
5 indifference, lack of concern
6 vexation, annoyance
7 anger
8 determination or loss of temper
9 he is joking or trying to attract somebody
10 anger or a threat

Exercise 2, page 247
1 a hard life
2 Don't stir up something which may cause trouble.
3 selfish. He has something which is no use to him but which he will not allow others to use.
4 deteriorated, become worse
5 very tired, exhausted
6 in an inferior position
7 You lucky person!
8 Every person has his or her time of glory or victory.
9 It rained heavily.
10 You have no chance at all, not even the slightest chance.

Exercise 3, page 247
1 She is very nervous about something which is about to happen. (She is not necessarily frightened but cannot sit still and wonders what will happen.)
2 That was a spiteful remark, intended to hurt somebody.
3 He is being used by somebody else and will get the blame if anything goes wrong.
4 You nearly gave our secret away.
5 The room is extremely small.
6 Let's wait and see what the result or decision is. It could be either way.
7 When the person in authority is away, the subordinates or younger ones will misbehave.
8 Even an ordinary person may at least look at a king, so don't be so proud.
9 A cat burglar is somebody who climbs up pipes to break into people's homes.
10 The audience booed the actors or performers.

Exercise 4, page 248
1 hidden, concealed (and probably illegal) payment
2 not in favour, under suspicion, regarded with disfavour by somebody
3 now being built

4 When people shoot at us, keep your head down (near the ground)
5 controlled by new people
6 in a tent
7 in the Armed Forces and carrying weapons
8 as a result of force or threats (not made voluntarily)
9 under the legal age (18 or 21, depending on the country) at which she can decide for herself
10 being investigated, with people enquiring into what he has said or done

Exercise 5, page 248
1 a special day, a holiday or day of importance to somebody
2 bureaucratic delay or the rules of bureaucracy
3 caught doing something wrong
4 something intended to deceive people, something irrelevant in a discussion
5 something which will certainly annoy a person
6 It made me very angry.
7 to show fear or cowardice
8 an expensive but useless gift
9 un untruthful remark made with good intentions to help or save somebody
10 the rejected member of a family or group

Exercise 6, page 248
1 to be in a bad mood or temper
2 to be quite right by finding a cause, factor, reason, etc. for something
3 to agree with a person
4 to do two things with one action or at the same time
5 to make an embarrassing or serious mistake
6 to be active in, or concerned with, too many different undertakings
7 to have a point which you wish to discuss or quarrel about with somebody
8 to feel something intuitively or by instinct
9 to do things in the wrong order
10 to start work seriously on something
11 to refrain from taking sides and to be ready to hear all the evidence before attempting to form a conclusion; to be objective
12 to punish somebody without following the law
13 to reverse the position so that you switch from an inferior to a superior position
14 to get revenge (by doing to somebody what they did to you)
15 to be frank and reveal your views, advantages, assets, etc., especially in negotiations
16 to be favoured (or disliked) by somebody
17 to make a point of avoiding a person
18 to receive more than you expected; often, to come off worse in a dispute
19 to do something quickly and without much difficulty
20 to disagree or not to obey or follow a person

Exercise 7, page 249
1 to pretend that you cannot see something
2 to pretend that you cannot hear what is said
3 to reform
4 when attacked, to allow somebody to continue with the attack; not to hit back
5 Please see Exercise 6, question 13, page 248.
6 to arrive at a meeting
7 to reject an offer
8 He did something for us. He obtained something we wanted.
9 He did not show any change of emotion. In particular, he was not frightened or surprised.
10 He changes his beliefs from one side to another. (This has a bad connotation.)

41

Exercise 8, page 249
1. exactly right
2. arrived exactly on time
3. arguing about something which cannot be altered
4. It is no longer observed by people.
5. He is waiting for people to die so that he can be promoted by stepping into their shoes.
6. to pay the bill
7. to be responsible for your own actions and upkeep
8. It is your turn to take action.
9. He is afraid to go ahead with some project.
10. He managed to do something well. He was lucky and found himself in a favourable situation.

Exercise 9, page 249
1. something (often an excuse) intended to deceive people
2. flattery
3. something which cannot be understood
4. not a real holiday at all because a person does on his holiday what he does every day at work
5. some obstacle which prevents people from proceeding with a scheme
6. a bad person
7. something saved up (usually money)
8. a source of trouble and therefore something to be avoided
9. an imaginary danger or situation (A mare does not have a nest.)

Exercise 10, page 250
1. It has no effect on him. This is often applied to criticism which a person ignores.
2. Family relationship is stronger than friendship with outsiders.
3. She is unsuitable for this work and unhappy in it.
4. He is not suitable for this work or situation. He does not fit in and perhaps cannot do the work properly.
5. It is not easy to survive financially when inflation is high.
6. You should adjust your expenditure to match your income.
7. You will get into trouble.
8. She bought something (bad) without having first examined it carefully.
9. We should make peace and stop arguing.
10. He is very much controlled or dominated by his wife.

Exercise 11, page 250
1. to be suspicious and think that something may be wrong
2. to rely too heavily on one project or thing
3. to deceive somebody
4. to attempt a most difficult task; to try to find something which is almost impossible to find
5. to face a problem or danger squarely and openly (instead of trying to ignore or avoid it)
6. to give somebody complete freedom of action. This is often used to mean 'to agree to pay whatever it may cost'
7. to take an inferior position
8. to make expenditure and income match
9. to try to do too many different things at the same time or to have so many different interests that one cannot do well in any of them
10. to lower somebody's position; to deflate a person, especially in an argument
11. to find a hidden or less obvious message or reason
12. to be cornered and prepared to fight

13 to do as well as you can with something which is not very good
14 to make economies; to spend less
15 to misunderstand a point or situation
16 to bribe somebody or pay to get something done quickly
17 to be an active competitor, to make somebody work hard to accomplish something
18 to be in a quarrel or dispute with a person
19 to be (a) insensitive to criticism, (b) sensitive and quick to react to criticism
20 to have some trick or method in reserve so that you can use it when necessary

62 Common errors

Exercise 1, page 251
1 agreeable, pleasant, enjoyable
2 organising
3 impressive
4 returning
5 ill
6 angrily
7 violent
8 show (reflect the fact that)
9 distinguish, differentiate
10 told, ordered (demanded that we)

Exercise 2, page 251
1 respond, reply
2 preceding
3 refrain
4 quite
5 quite
6 hostel
7 scored
8 alternately
9 ensure
10 affect

Exercise 3, page 252
1 an outbreak
2 overtake
3 non-flammable
4 arouse
5 route
6 earn
7 notify
8 watch
9 attracts
10 endangers

Exercise 4, page 252
1 write
2 may be
3 relinquish, give up
4 expect
5 reduce, lower
6 attract
7 punishment
8 final, last
9 remember
10 as a result of

Exercise 5, page 253
1 recognise
2 knocked
3 hit
4 tolerate
5 pay
6 devotes
7 expect, require
8 flaw
9 relieved
10 little

Exercise 6, page 253
1 recommend
2 There
3 up
4 machines
5 keep, maintain
6 made
7 person running, proprietor
8 modern, contemporary
9 In the old days, formerly
10 bunch, bouquet

Part 5: Language practice

63 Word formation and parts of speech

Exercise 1, page 257
1. length
2. heat
3. conclusion
4. destruction
5. explosion
6. simplicity
7. provision
8. deterrent
9. Briton
10. narrator, narration
11. reality, realism
12. guardian
13. ability
14. alteration
15. engraving
16. falsehood
17. pronunciation
18. explanation
19. inferiority
20. breadth

Exercise 2, page 257
1. This depends on the situation. If we refer to the thing as a single unit, we use a singular verb. If we are thinking of the separate parts of the thing, we use a plural verb.
2. No.
3. Most do. Some don't, e.g. furniture, luggage and similar words, unless we call these collective nouns.
4. No article at all if the noun is not qualified.

Exercise 3, page 258
1. tomatoes
2. photos
3. radios
4. mangoes
5. donkeys
6. chairmen
7. indices, -exes
8. stories
9. storeys
10. theories
11. mouthfuls
12. lives
13. antennae
14. museums
15. pendulums
16. curricula, -ums
17. octopuses
18. parents
19. daughters-in-law
20. Smiths

Exercise 4, page 259
1. dangerous
2. comforting, comfortable
3. brutal
4. suburban
5. buoyant
6. circular
7. legendary
8. boiling, boiled
9. frozen, freezing
10. absent
11. statuesque
12. useful, used, useless
13. racist, racing, raced
14. horrible
15. cubic
16. musical
17. walking
18. vicious
19. foolish
20. created, creating, creative
21. sensible, sensitive
22. childlike, childish
23. brotherly
24. ominous

Exercise 5, page 260
1. enflame
2. deepen
3. widen
4. horrify
5. believe
6. enjoy
7. sharpen
8. threaten
9. solidify
10. naturalise
11. generalise
12. engulf
13. kneel
14. purify
15. popularise

Exercise 6, page 260
1. explosion
2. pronunciation
3. explanation
4. annoyance
5. agreement
6. listener
7. description
8. provision
9. robber, robbery
10. burglar(y)
11. seizure
12. choice
13. knowledge
14. applicant, application
15. behaviour
16. carriage
17. clearance
18. decision
19. delivery
20. enclosure

Exercise 7, page 261
1 making, widen
2 starving, hungrily
3 driving, loss
4 beautifully, practise, hard, takes
5 stealing, allegation, borrowed, temporarily
6 getting, cancellation, waiting
7 luckily, collision, parked, gradually
8 hurriedly, pouring, excited, screaming
9 endurance, fitness, successful, usually
10 Impatience, carelessness, punishment, unlikely, drastically

64 Adjectives

Exercise 1, page 264
1 concerned
2 reserved
3 exciting
4 necessarily
5 bright blue
6 sarcastic
7 answer expected
8 sleepy
9 completely
10 accurately
11 very grateful
12 a rational and inexpensive one

Exercise 2, page 264
1 was too lazy
2 impossible
3 badly
4 the poor
5 examples below
6 easy
7 previously
8 sweet
9 are jealous
10 industrial
11 economic
12 sad

Exercise 3, page 265
1 unwelcome
2 shirt
3 peaceful
4 trifling
5 unacceptable
6 no pain
7 He is injured
8 elegant
9 Don't be afraid
10 light green in colour, a light green colour
11 unconscious
12 small white

Exercise 4, page 265
1 critical and surprising,
2 honest and able
3 noisily (? jokingly)
4 abundance
5 oppressed and ill-treated
6 cautious
7 anxious
8 imaginative
9 suspicion
10 greatly
11 strong-willed
12 psychological

Exercise 5, page 266
1 You must be silent in the library.
2 He succeeded in persuading her to go.
3 Peter's absence was not noticed by anybody.
4 They found the long journey tiring.
5 It was difficult for us to find your address.
6 He is a well-known athlete.
7 We found the news very surprising.
8 The lorry was behind the taxi.
9 We were informed of the results by a friend.
10 Although it was a cloudy day, we decided to go for a picnic.
11 Peter asked us where we were going the next day.
12 My friend suggested that we (should) go for a walk.

65 Agreement

Exercise 1, page 268
1. they sometimes take
2. live
3. has
4. he should go
5. be respectable men or women
6. we were surprised, were white
7. has
8. is increasing
9. has been
10. knows that
11. was painted
12. future is hopeless

Exercise 2, page 270
1. have, have (because of 'their' later in the sentence)
2. has (because of 'its' later in the sentence)
3. have (influenced by 'shopkeepers')
4. is (influenced by 'group')
5. are
6. are
7. is
8. is
9. is, is
10. are
11. say, is
12. wants, likes

Exercise 3, page 271
1. are, are
2. likes, arises
3. need, is
4. are
5. is
6. are
7. is/are
8. takes
9. are
10. is
11. are
12. are

Exercise 4, page 271
1. keep them away
2. does not worry
3. starts work
4. was discovered
5. these lifts
6. dare not
7. is exported
8. is
9. has increased
10. was bad
11. as good citizens
12. as students,

Exercise 5, page 272
1. are, are
2. are, is
3. has, is
4. spread
5. is, has, is
6. are
7. was, was
8. are, is
9. is, is
10. has, is
11. has, is
12. is (will be)

66 Articles

Exercise 1, page 273
1. a
2. a
3. an
4. a, an
5. an
6. a, a
7. an/the
8. an, a
9. an, an
10. an, an
11. an
12. a

Exercise 2, page 275
1. It is hard
2. At first sight
3. for educated people
4. make better
5. is slang
6. encourages customers
7. even to native-speakers
8. get fresh air
9. brought loud applause
10. all people

Exercise 3, page 275

1. in the human
2. in the Chinese
3. save a great
4. are a real
5. *television, has a bad
6. at the City Hall
7. as a cucumber
8. After a lengthy discussion
9. the/a newspaper
10. when the sex

*'Television' is a comparatively new word and its use has not yet been fixed. Thus we can say 'the television' or 'television' (without an article) in sentence 5.

Exercise 4, page 276

1. under the influence
2. led to a serious
3. get a chance
4. to a certain extent
5. use a simile
6. on the next page
7. keep on the alert
8. Talking on the telephone
9. Throughout the ages
10. half an hour

Exercise 5, page 276

1. the same rules
2. an island
3. has a very
4. a word for word
5. for a picnic
6. a university
7. having supper
8. an alarming
9. despite the efforts
10. by electricity

67 Cloze passages

In many cases, alternatives are possible. Not all alternatives are included below.

Exercise 1, page 279

1. romantic
2. ago
3. thinking, hoping, believing
4. listen
5. him
6. well, smoothly, efficiently
7. that, because, when, since, as
8. another
9. completely
10. took, carried, sent
11. complained, spoke
12. assistant, electrician
13. was
14. the
15. with
16. a
17. it
18. Did
19. when, after
20. said, replied

Exercise 2, page 279

1. go, get
2. discovered, found
3. ice
4. relieve, stop, lessen, reduce, remove
5. cubes
6. hand
7. the
8. index
9. this
10. notice, find, see, discover
11. pain, ache
12. per
13. discovered, found
14. used, studied
15. at
16. all
17. shown, taught, told
18. were, remained
19. discovered, realised, admitted, agreed, found
20. relieved, stopped, reduced

47

Exercise 3, page 280

1. samples/sent (were)
2. journey/a (took)
3. problem,/hospital (the)
4. /experiment (an)
5. /were (which, that)
6. proved/be (to)
7. cheaply/efficiently (and)
8. doctors/to (plan, want)
9. representatives/several (of, from)
10. about/new (the)

Exercise 4, page 280

1. the/of (price, cost)
2. /further (were)
3. because/inflation (of)
4. countries/had (and)
5. others/lacked (that, which)
6. to/oil (buy, use)
7. In/cases (some, several)
8. alcohol/produced (was, is)
9. was/and (imported, bought)
10. thus/foreign (saving)

68 Comparison

Exercise 1, page 284

1. larger
2. more dangerous
3. more valuable, harder
4. more honest, more talkative
5. the largest
6. most vital
7. more powerful, more destructive
8. older
9. worse, more serious, greater
10. *faster, safer, more expensive
11. the most pleasant, the best
12. stronger, better

*In (10) we can use 'more dangerous' or 'safer'. There are no reliable statistics on this point. It depends whether you measure total distance or the number of journeys made.

Exercise 2, page 284

1. more, less
2. more, less
3. more, more
4. the most, the least
5. more, less
6. the most
7. more, the least
8. More, less
9. the most, the least
10. less

Exercise 3, page 285

1. to a bigger house
2. the most difficult
3. than it is
4. than that of a farmer
5. worse
6. and more natural
7. It is much easier
8. The worst thing in my country
9. Mary is my best friend
10. was worse

69 Conditionals and 'If'

Exercise 1, page 286

1. Mummy will be delighted.
2. where shall we go?
3. we won't be able to go to school.
4. take a message for me.
5. post these letters for me and get some stamps.

6 many buildings will collapse and thousands of people will be killed.
7 there will be protests, demonstrations and all sorts of trouble.
8 everybody will be delighted.
9 how many people will survive?
10 I'll pay it back at the end of the month.

Exercise 2, page 287
1 many young men would want to join the Police Force.
2 there would be fewer accidents.
3 I would put it all in a bank and then think about it.
4 I would try to put more emphasis on moral education.
5 perhaps all countries would combine to drive them out.
6 many businesses would collapse.
7 I would choose the U.S.A. or Canada.
8 you would get much better results.
9 I would take it to a police station.
10 I would try to get admitted to a university in California or Australia because I like warm weather.

Exercise 3, page 290
1 Peter asked me whether I had found my watch.
2 Peter asked whether it would rain the next day.
3 The lady asked me whether I understood English.
4 We asked the police inspector whether we could enter the building.
5 The inspector asked us whether we had any relatives living there.
6 Susan asked me whether I was going to John's wedding the following Saturday.
7 The tourist asked me whether the Rex Hotel was a good one.
8 The lady asked me whether I could drive a car.
9 The policeman asked us whether we had seen the accident happen.
10 Anne asked whether it was raining and whether the Sports Meeting would be cancelled.

70 Connectives

Exercise 1, page 292
1 traffic was diverted.
2 there are also more criminals.
3 I decided not to buy it.
4 don't buy them.
5 I couldn't cross the road to talk to Peter.
6 I think television does much more good than harm.
7 ships had to sail right round the Cape of Good Hope.
8 I often see different kinds of ships.
9 we decided not to go swimming
10 there will eventually be a major war or serious famine.

Exercise 2, page 295
1 Despite
2 Moreover, Besides
3 However, Nevertheless
4 Nor, Neither; Above all, In particular
5 Besides, In addition, Moreover; However

6 Undoubtedly, For example; Besides, Moreover, In addition; However, Nevertheless, Even so
7 and, but; However
8 thus, thereby; As a result, Consequently; In addition
9 However; Nevertheless, Even so
10 nor, neither; However; As a result of

71 Future action

Exercise 1, page 297
1 will decide
2 will not increase
3 will be put out
4 will come, will be coming
5 will be met
6 will be promoted
7 will be
8 will be
9 will leave
10 will take
11 will win
12 will you see

Exercise 3, page 299
1 correct
2 correct
3 closed
4 Shall we
5 correct
6 It will
7 correct
8 improve, when she has
9 arrive OR have arrived
10 will be blocked
11 correct
12 correct

72 Gerunds

Exercise 1, page 300
1 meeting, seeing
2 speaking, talking
3 taking, borrowing, stealing
4 preparing, cooking
5 moving, going, transferring
6 getting, finding, taking
7 paying, raising, reducing
8 collecting, studying
9 putting
10 driving, repairing, pushing
11 smoking, dancing, drinking, gambling
12 understanding, knowing, caring
13 borrowing; lending
14 thinking; talking
15 approaching, entering
16 failing, forgetting
17 meeting, seeing, welcoming
18 solving
19 having, keeping; keeping, driving
20 drinking, smoking, over-eating

Exercise 2, page 301
1 playing, being; keeping
2 finding, locating; making
3 having, getting
4 posting; buying
5 hurting; sending
6 going; entering
7 listening; growing
8 stealing; consulting
9 criticising; making
10 arriving
11 driving, speaking, standing; driving
12 going; meeting, seeing
13 opening
14 making; disturbing
15 hearing, learning
16 checking; making
17 thanking; allowing
18 getting, obtaining
19 buying, having
20 winning; insisting, saying

Exercise 3, page 302
There are too many alternatives to give them all here.

1. playing, chatting, going for a swim, having a picnic
2. collecting stamps, making dresses, cooking their own food
3. drinking beer, smoking cigars, eating too much
4. having stolen the money, stealing the money, driving recklessly
5. making that dress, repairing the radio, replying to John
6. putting them down, having them a few minutes ago
7. talking, making a noise, arguing, phoning him
8. meeting Mary, going to the airport, going out
9. dreaming, talking, wasting your time
10. keeping, retaining, having, repairing
11. having to stand, sitting at the front
12. writing, posting, answering, sending
13. going to evening classes, getting up earlier
14. buying, getting, having
15. arguing with him, living very long with him
16. giving, deciding on, announcing
17. dieting; eating only vegetables
18. walking; sitting on a cold bus
19. shooting, heading, passing the ball, dribbling
20. feeling sorry, thinking how lucky I am, being suspicious

73 Indirect (reported) speech

Exercise 2, page 307
1. She told me to shut the door quietly.
2. She asked me to get some rice and fish for her.
3. He warned us to keep away from the wet paint.
4. She told me to put the keys in her bag.
5. She reminded me to bring my money the next day.
6. He told me to put my books away and turn the light off.
7. I told him not to leave his shoes by the door.
8. He told me not to forget to bring my fees the next day.
9. She asked us not to be angry with her.
10. He told us not to pay any attention to the rumours about him.

Exercise 3, page 308
1. begged (asked, requested, urged)
2. reminded
3. advised
4. urged (begged, advised, asked)
5. begged
6. advised, asked; advised, ordered
7. told, reminded
8. asked, requested, ordered
9. asked, requested, told
10. advised, told, asked

Exercise 4, page 308
1. Mary said she had left my camera in her house.
2. My uncle told me that more than sixty huts had been destroyed in the fire yesterday morning. (were)
3. Mrs Lee said she felt sorry for me.
4. The policeman said that I must take my driving licence to the Central police station the following morning.

5 The man said that he had come to check the telephone. He said that somebody had complained that it was out of order.
6 My friend said that he would come at about seven yesterday evening and would bring Mary's photos with him.
7 The fire officer told us that the fire had started in the kitchen of the hotel.
8 The girl said she was waiting for her friend who was in a camera shop.
9 Somebody told me that all the tickets for the concert had been sold already.

Exercise 5, page 309

1   Mummy,
Somebody from the Speedy Bookshop phoned to say the books you ordered have arrived. You can pick them up at any time.
Anne

2   John,
Mary phoned and wanted to speak to you. She asked me to tell you that her brother told her you have been chosen to play football for the school first team.
Tom

3   Mary,
Peter Brown phoned to say there is a job going at the Southland Bank in Market Street. They want somebody in their Credit Office. His uncle is the manager. Could you please phone Peter if you are interested in the job. His number is 4498042.
Sue

4   Peter,
John Dilena phoned to speak to you. He says he's going into town tomorrow morning and will be happy to give you a lift if you want to go with him. Could you please phone him at 8347221.
Margaret

5   Daddy,
Mr Frank Wilson phoned. He said he has an appointment at your office at 9.30 am tomorrow but he has to cancel it because his wife is very ill. It's not serious. He said he'll phone you at the office during the morning.
John

6   Daddy,
Somebody from the Newville Insurance Company phoned. Your car insurance policy expires today. The man said he had sent you a renewal notice but hadn't received a reply. He wants to know if you want to renew the policy or not. His telephone number is 4103047.
Anne

74 Indirect (reported) questions

Exercise 1, page 311

A question mark is needed after numbers 3, 5, 7, 9, 15, 17 and 18. A full stop is needed after the other sentences.

Exercise 2, page 312

She asked me... (The tense of reported verbs depends on the situation, and in this exercise we do not know the exact situation.)

1   what my name was/is.
2   how much oranges cost.
3   where my sister was/is.

4 what time the concert started/starts.
5 how many eggs I wanted/want.
6 when Peter is/was going to sell his motorcycle.
7 how she could get to the market.
8 why I wanted to see the manager.
9 where my brother had found the money.
10 how long it would take her to get to the railway station.
11 why I had not replied to David's letter
12 when I am going to move to Canada.

Exercise 3, page 312

He asked me whether…

1 I was thirsty.
2 I was/am over eighteen.
3 my brother is still in England.
4 he was in my way.
5 Mary was at home then.
6 there is/was much traffic at night.
7 anybody had been seriously injured in the accident.
8 I had been absent the day before he spoke.
9 he was the first to arrive.
10 I was in charge of the maintenance department.

Exercise 4, page 313

1 Susan asked me whether Mary could play the guitar.
2 John asked Anne whether her brother liked acting.
3 My mother asked me whether I had finished all my work9 yet.
4 My uncle asked me whether Susan had got a job yet.
5 David asked me whether I would like to join the Photography Club.
6 My brother asked me whether it would rain on Sunday.
7 Mary asked me whether I knew Peter's telephone number.
8 I asked John whether he had found his keys yet.
9 The manager asked me whether I had brought my testimonials with me.
10 John asked me whether I had been to the cinema recently.

Exercise 5, page 313

1 … where my bicycle was.
2 where they were when
3 how a small insect could carry
4 is how the words are used.
5 why I should learn
6 where the police station is.
7 why they couldn't line up
8 where the X-ray department was
9 what rain is.
10 why you don't believe me.
11 singing.
12 why you were late

75 Infinitives

Exercise 1, page 315

1 play
2 listen
3 have, eat, drink
4 leave, put
5 start, cause
6 repair, look at
7 be
8 turn, switch

Exercise 2, page 316

1 stay, remain
2 enter
3 touch, handle
4 live
5 play
6 climb
7 discuss, debate
8 get; go; come
9 wait
10 listen; to answer
11 to move
12 (to) repair
13 tell
14 take
15 have
16 borrow
17 keep, save
18 bite, sting
19 try, take
20 go

Exercise 4, page 318

1	to enter	4	to be caught	7	to learn	10	to be chosen
2	to hear	5	to light	8	to arrive	11	to get; to be given
3	to meet	6	to fly	9	to have/hold	12	to put/invest

Exercise 5, page 319

1 You must get a new one.
2 You must wear your best clothes.
3 We must be careful with it.
4 I must get a present for him.
5 You should shut it.
6 He ought to stop.
7 I must be home by nine.
8 He should see a dentist.
9 You ought to boil it.
10 You ought to improve it.

Exercise 6, page 319

1 There are some serious problems for you to consider.
2 There are some serious problems for us to solve at the meeting in Tokyo tomorrow.
3 Here are some invoices for you to check.
4 Here is a bill to be checked.
5 There are two more building sites to be sold at auction next month.
6 Here are some shirts for you to repair.
7 There are at least sixty thousand scripts to be marked in this examination.
8 There is another candidate for us to interview.
9 Here is a book for you to read.
10 There are many advantages to be considered.

Exercise 7, page 321

1	the man say	5	easy to carry	9	let us get		
2	easy to use	6	man walk across	10	may be arrested		
3	spending	7	will be promoted	11	worth pointing out		
4	must be kept	8	except wait	12	ability to become		

76 Participles

Exercise 1, page 323

1 repairing
2 working
3 climbing, barking
4 talking
5 going
6 waiting
7 discussing
8 coming
9 speaking, talking
10 rescuing

Exercise 2, page 324

1 sitting behind Anne
2 parked over there
3 made in Japan
4 living in rural areas
5 waving to Peter
6 singing in the trees
7 destroyed during the floods
8 CAUGHT STEALING
9 sent off in the first half
10 standing by the coach

Exercise 3, page 324

1 Not realising that it was five o'clock, John got out of bed.
2 Feeling rather tired, Mary decided to have a rest.
3 Hoping to catch the bus, I ran as fast as I could.

4 Thinking that it was going to rain, Mr Brown took an umbrella with him.
5 Not realising that the telephone was out of order, I tried to telephone my brother.
6 Opening the door quietly, Mary tip-toed into the room.

Exercise 4, page 325

2 wallet, wondering
3 path, hoping
5 frowned, knowing
6 frowned, suspecting
10 lady, hoping
11 shop, not
12 road, narrowly

Exercise 5, page 326

1 Having lost
2 Having been cheated
3 having been told
4 having lived
5 having flown
6 Having been warned
7 Having finished
8 having been
9 having missed
10 Having waited

77 Prepositions

Exercise 1, page 327

1 arrived on
2 storm last
3 begins next
4 is on 31st
5 her last
6 flat in 1982
7 humid in
8 Next Sunday
9 do on Saturday
10 party on Tuesday

Exercise 2, page 328

Omit the following words:

1 to
2 with
3 into
4 about
5 back
6 away
7 about
8 with
9 in
10 to
11 for
12 to
13 to
14 back
15 in
16 in
17 to
18 with

Exercise 3, page 328

Omit the following words:

1 of
2 out
3 for
4 to
5 out
6 to
7 down
8 out
9 about
10 down
11 up
12 to
13 for
14 for
15 for
16 to
17 in
18 for

Exercise 4, page 330

1 –
2 –
3 in
4 with
5 –
6 –
7 towards
8 on
9 –,-
10 –
11 –
12 –
13 on
14 of
15 with
16 –
17 –
18 –
19 from
20 between

55

Exercise 5, page 333
1. below, above
2. below
3. about, between/amongst
4. of, in
5. before
6. in, of, throughout
7. In, with, at, on, of, at
8. Of, –
9. at, without
10. to, to

Exercise 6, page 334
1. in a quiet corner
2. succeeded in persuading
3. a definition of many
4. candles out at
5. for boys than for
6. interest in trade
7. catch it at the last
8. Early one morning
9. sincere in her belief
10. speakers of the main
11. instead of foreign ones
12. objects to the use of
13. keep up with him (for) most
14. experiment with his language
15. exceeds this level
16. did not end until
17. demanding a 15 per cent
18. revert to the owner
19. lack skill
20. recording the score

Exercise 7, page 339
1. into, with
2. at/on
3. In, to/for
4. of, at, on, in, of
5. against, with, to
6. without
7. of, on
8. in, in
9. from, into, for, in, of
10. to, at, on, in, in
11. Beyond, of, on
12. at, on, up, on

78 Pronouns

Exercise 1, page 340
1. listens to it
2. friend and I
3. we must keep
4. save him or her
5. ate it all
6. Omit 'them'.
7. on them
8. between him and me
9. It was I *or* It was me
10. My friend and I
11. informing her that
12. and it is still
13. look after them when
14. write them down
15. they leave, they gradually forget, they have learnt

Exercise 3, page 342
1. yourself
2. myself
3. themselves
4. yourself
5. themselves
6. himself
7. yourselves, yourselves
8. itself
9. myself
10. oneself
11. myself
12. yourselves
13. himself
14. themselves
15. ourselves

Exercise 3, page 343
1. Where is the key which opens this cupboard?
2. That is the man who sold me the watch.
3. I'll speak to the lady who owns the shop.
4. Do you know the girl who is standing next to Mary?
5. Some men have built a car which runs on solar energy.
6. I think this is the path that leads to the river.
7. Rabies is a disease which can be fatal to human beings.

8 Is this the train that goes to London?
9 What happened to the cow that escaped from some men and ran through the streets?
10 Soldiers will soon recapture the prisoners who escaped from prison during the night.
11 That is the tree that is dangerous and should be cut down.
12 I don't know the name of the lady who gave away the prizes.

Exercise 4, page 344

1 who is talking to Anne
2 which is coming from Manchester
3 who enters that building
4 which destroyed the cinema
5 who reported the accident
6 which opens this cupboard
7 who live in glass houses
8 who hesitates
9 who spoke to you
10 which are ten years old
11 who smoke
12 which leads to Tom's village

79 Punctuation

Exercise 1, page 348

1 I saw Mary, Anne, Susan and Margaret at the wedding last Saturday.
2 with. It
3 Mr Brown is an engineer. He works in a factory. However, he is also a very good painter.
4 John is a very pleasant and helpful boy, not a bit like his father. I quite like him. (Or use a dash instead of a comma after 'boy'.)
5 quietly. That is
6 of bed. Then I
7 The sky grew darker and darker. The wind increased in strength, blowing all the papers off the table.
8 The need for coats is limited in this area, for the winter is not very cold, as it is elsewhere. (Alternatives are possible.)
9 My sister hopes to be a social worker when she is older. She wants to go to a university. OR
My sister hopes to be a social worker. When she is older, she wants to go to a university.
10 After the operation, Peter could not eat or sleep very well. A short walk made him feel faint, so he often had to rest.

Exercise 2, page 351

1 the walls of the building
2 the meaning of the sentence
3 the attention of the class
4 the influence of drama
5 the wheels of the car
6 the number of the licence
7 the truth of the saying
8 the roof of the hut
9 the life of a town
10 the cause of the fire

Exercise 3, page 351

1 Draw a circle with a diameter of 12cm and calculate its area.
2 You can use somebody else's book, Peter, if yours is at home.
3 I can hear the birds singing, can't you?
4 Next week we'll get two days' holiday.
5 One should always try to keep one's word. Don't you agree, Mary?
6 The discovery of oil off the coast of our country will certainly increase its prosperity. There is no doubt of this.

7 One should be ready to defend one's country when it is attacked by its enemies.
8 There will be a children's concert at the community centre on Saturday.
9 In science fiction, the writer's creative ability can make a book very successful.
10 Did you go to Peter and Mary's wedding, David?

Exercise 4, page 353

1 Mary said, 'If it rains, the Sports Meeting will be cancelled. Then it may be held next week.' (*or* do not put capital letters on 'sports meeting'.)
2 'If there is a storm,' Mary said, 'the concert will be postponed until next Saturday.'
3 There was a severe storm. Peter told us the final match was abandoned. It will be played next Monday.
4 My friend told me that the game had been cancelled because of the rain. He said that the game might be played later.
5 'Excuse me,' the stranger said, 'could you tell me where the nearest police station is?'
Mary gave the man directions and then said, 'You'd better go by taxi. There's a taxi rank just over there.'
'Many thanks,' the man said. He turned and walked across the road to get a taxi. (we can start a new paragraph at 'He turned…')
6 'I wonder if you'd do me a favour,' Peter asked his sister.
'Certainly,' she replied. 'What is it?'
'I've got to go out,' Peter said, 'but I'm expecting a phone call from David. If he phones, would you mind taking a message for me?'
'No problem,' Anne said.
7 The sales assistant told me that he did not know when the manager would be back. He did not know where he had gone.
8 'I don't know where the manager has gone,' the salesman said, 'and I don't know when he'll be back. Sorry I can't help you.'
(Or: Sorry. I can't help you.')
9 'We must find out which plane Uncle is arriving on,' my mother said. 'Then we can phone the airport and find out if it's on time.'
10 'Does your brother still work in a bank?' Mary asked me.
'Yes,' I said. 'He's an assistant manager now. He was promoted after he passed the final exam of the Institute of Bankers.'
'Oh, that's good news!' Mary said. 'Do congratulate him for me when you see him.'

80 Spelling

Exercise 1, page 355

1 receive
2 deceitful
3 weight
4 height
5 believe
6 conceited
7 field
8 friend
9 received
10 their
11 ceiling
12 freight

Exercise 2, page 355

1 occurred
2 omitted
3 SMOKING
4 digging
5 admitted
6 planning
7 referred
8 committed
9 beginning
10 shopping

81 Verbs: present tenses

Exercise 1, page 360
1. does not vary
2. has
3. does not come
4. reads, watches
5. cause, cost
6. knows, moves
7. Does … live
8. Do … belong
9. do … stay
10. follow
11. comes
12. wastes, makes
13. knows
14. live
15. stops, get

Exercise 2, page 361
1. are stolen, are recovered, are exported, (are) sold. (Omit the last 'are'.)
2. is searched, are found
3. are not taken
4. are taken, bought, are washed, are sold, are thrown
5. is collected, stored, is needed, is taken, treated, are added, removed, is pumped

Exercise 3, page 361
1. consists, is believed
2. belongs, is cleaned, looks
3. exists, are caused
4. leave, are inspected, do not contain, are rejected, enquire, are made
5. are inspected, repaired, overhauled, have, thinks, recommends
6. does . . . arrive, is expected, is not delayed
7. happen, are caused, occur, seems
8. are advised, are warned, have
9. sheds, fall, are broken, are turned, reach, rely
10. works, are promoted, hopes

Exercise 4, page 364
1. wants, don't know, wants
2. is being repaired
3. is washing
4. has, thinks
5. are exported, are needed, is being built
6. is kept, are stored, has, expect, has
7. are searching, are being drilled, are investigating
8. is being done, face, presents, is being considered, are being made

82 Verbs: past actions

Exercise 1, page 367
1. has taken, has been stolen
2. have been made, have managed, has been achieved
3. have you done, haven't seen, haven't touched
4. has sunk, have been seen, has been rescued, has gone
5. have been trying, have not succeeded, have been refused, have failed
6. have you been working, Have you been promoted
7. has borrowed, Have you got

59

8 has happened, has had
9 has been checked, have confirmed, have received
10 have been looking, have finished

Exercise 2, page 368

1 (a) 've been
  (b) went
2 (a) 've read
  (b) read
3 (a) has borrowed
  (b) borrowed
4 (a) knocked
  (b) has been
5 (a) had
  (b) haven't had

Exercise 3, page 371

Various sentences are possible. The verb forms are:

1	blew	6	felt	11	meant	16	understood
2	met	7	lent	12	slid	17	drove
3	taught	8	flowed	13	spent	18	fell
4	struck	9	complained	14	split	19	stole
5	dug	10	destroyed	15	arose	20	woke

Exercise 4, page 371

1 exploded, were, rose, blew, was brought, (were) extinguished, flowed, found
2 rose, fell, reached, created, cost, (was) increased, raised, made
3 spent, was, was, slipped, slid, threw, built, did not like, shivered, wore
4 came, went, wanted, found, bargained, drove, took, left, wrote, stopped, took, said, was made, thought
5 was taken, put, did not stick, drank, felt, got

Exercise 5, page 373

1 He said (that) he had finished cleaning the car.
2 She told us she had lost her bracelet the previous Saturday.
3 I thought I had lost all my money.
4 Mary asked me if I had seen Peter.
5 Anne asked me whether my father had sold his car.
6 I told her he had not sold it yet.
7 My friend asked me how long I had been waiting.
8 I told him I had been there half an hour at least.
9 John said his bicycle had been stolen.
10 We told him that the thief had been caught ten minutes earlier.

Exercise 6, page 374

1 realised, had left
2 did not know, had gone
3 warned, had been knocked
4 had gone, started
5 decided, had been
6 had planted, watered
7 denied, had driven
8 wished, had worked
9 admitted, had made
10 found, had been looking